# The Ultimate Homeschool Physical Education Game Book

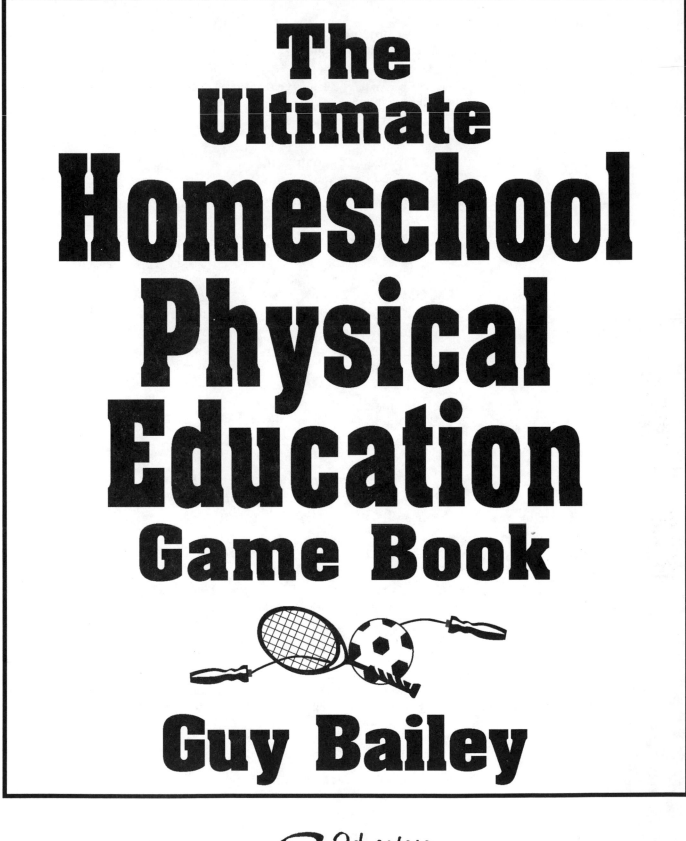

## Guy Bailey

Educators Press
Camas Washington

ISBN: 0-9669727-4-0
Publisher's Cataloging-in-Publication
(*Provided by Quality Books, Inc.*)


Bailey, Guy, 1956-
      The ultimate homeschool physical education game book
: fun & easy-to-use games & activities to help you teach
your children fitness, movement & sport skills/ Guy
Bailey, -- 1st ed.
      p.cm.
      Includes index.
      LCCN 2002093722
      ISBN 0-9669727-4-0

      1.   Physical education for children—Study and
teaching—Activity programs.  2. Home schooling.
3. Games.  I. Title.


GV361.B24 2003              796.077
                                        QBI02-200619

The author and publisher assume that the reader will teach these games using professional judgment and
respect for student safety. In regards to this statement, the author and publisher shall have neither liability
nor responsibility in the case of injury to anyone participating in the activities contained within.

**EDUCATORS PRESS**
5333 NE Jackson Street
Camas, WA  98607
(360) 834-3049
www.educatorspress.com

Printed in the United States of America

# Acknowledgments

I want to thank the many dedicated homeschooling parents I have had the pleasure of working with over the course of my career. Your questions and concerns about providing a quality home-based physical education experience for your children provided the inspiration for this book.

A special thanks goes out to all my colleagues in the physical education profession. Because some of the game ideas contained in this resource have been collected from attending workshops and conventions for over two decades, it is impossible to give specific game credit. However, I have learned so much from you in our sharing of ideas and teaching methodology over the years. Your professional advice, enthusiasm, and dedication to improving the health and fitness of our children is much appreciated.

I am especially indebted to Cynthia Wilson for her time and many contributions toward the crafting of this book. Her diagrams, illustrations, formatting, and book design advice was invaluable.

Finally, an author's family is always owed the greatest amount of gratitude, for they're the ones who make the biggest sacrifices. A special "Thank-you!" goes to my wife, Shelby, for her understanding, encouragement, and support.

*This book is dedicated to my family—my wife, Shelby whom I love and treasure,*
*and my three beautiful children, Justin, Austin, and Heather.*
*God has truly blessed me!*

"People ought to exercise every day…yet, more than a third of our children don't get an hour's worth of exercise in a week. How about parents playing a game with their children in the backyard for 30 minutes or an hour? It would be good for the child, it would be good for the parent, and it's good for the family."

*President George W. Bush*

# About the Author

**Guy Bailey**, M.Ed., is a physical education specialist at Mill Plain Elementary School in Vancouver, Washington. His educational background includes having a B.S. degree (Central Washington University), and a M.S. degree (Portland State University) in his specialty area of health and physical education. Guy has over 22 years of experience teaching physical education at the K-8 grade level, coaching youth sports, and directing after school sport activities. During this time, he has also counseled numerous parents of homeschooled children concerning appropriate physical education activities for the home setting.

In addition to this book, Guy has authored two other popular books on physical education. *The Ultimate Playground & Recess Game Book* (Educators Press, 2001) is a unique resource of over 170 playground and recess activities for K-8 grade children. *The Ultimate Sport Lead-Up Game Book* (Educators Press, 2001) is widely considered the most complete and comprehensive resource of games used to develop sport skills.

As a physical educator, Guy's professional goal is to equip each of his students with a love of movement and the basic skills needed to participate in an active lifestyle now and as adults. He believes that for lasting skill learning to take place, physical education needs to consist of success-oriented learning experiences that literally leave children craving for more. This book reflects Guy's philosophy of using activities that are not only skill based, but fun and meaningful as well.

In addition to his teaching and writing, Guy is actively involved in promoting literacy among elementary-age children. He has spoken at school assemblies, and worked with various groups on motivating children to read and write. He has also worked with the students in his own school on how to become young authors.

Guy and his wife, Shelby, reside in Camas, Washington. He has two sons, Justin and Austin, and a daughter, Heather. In his spare time, he enjoys reading, writing, jogging, weightlifting, fishing, and hiking the various trails in the beautiful Columbia River Gorge near his home. He also has a passion for college athletics and is a frequent visitor to college stadiums and gymnasiums throughout the Pacific Northwest.

**"Youngsters are most likely to develop physically active lifestyles if they are provided with physical activity experiences they enjoy and with which they can be successful."**

*Dr. Russell Pate*
*(President's Council on Physical Fitness & Sports)*

# PREFACE

*"Mr. Bailey, are there P.E. games we can play with our children at home that are fun, easy to teach, and do not require a gym or expensive equipment?"*

It was parent requests such as the one above that created the motivation for the birth of this book. During my 22 years of teaching physical education in the public schools, it's been a common practice for homechooling parents to bring their children to school for my physical education class. Many of the parents would stay and observe so they could repeat the instructional process at home on the non-class days. However, the instructional process for twenty-five students, conducted in a large gymnasium, is much different than what's needed for the home setting with just a few participants. At their request, I started advising homeschooling families on instructional activities specifically designed for the home setting that contained educational learning objectives, did not require a gymnasium or expensive equipment, involved only two to four participants, were easy to teach, and contained an element of fun for children.

Although I didn't realize it at the time, my homeschool game modifications changed how I taught physical education. I found that *all* of my students, not just the homeschooled students, preferred the games that were oriented toward partner and small group participation. Unlike many of the traditional, large-group activities, my "homeschool" games had students actively involved 100% of the time in learning, playing, and moving. These games didn't exclude kids or require long stretches of waiting and standing around. The level of skill development among my students was significantly enhanced with the introduction of these new learning experiences. Additionally, these changes presented opportunities for children to be successful and to feel good about themselves. As they became better skilled performers, their motivation to participate in exercise and healthy recreational activities outside the physical education setting increased as well. These small group games, with their emphasis on maximizing participation, are now the core of my physical education program.

*The Ultimate Homeschool Physical Education Game Book* is the ideal curriculum supplement to a broad-based home physical education program. My intention for this book is to provide home educators with a large selection of games that can be used to help their children develop specific physical education skills, and to get children excited about playing. However, these games are also adaptable for use outside the home setting, and for groups of any size. As mentioned, I have had large classes of children play these games successfully in small groups or in pairs. Therefore, I expect this book to have great appeal to a variety of professionals. In addition to the home educator, the game ideas presented here will benefit public and private school teachers, youth recreational leaders, camp counselors, youth church leaders, youth coaches, scout leaders, day care personnel, and just about anyone who works with children.

Physical education games make a valuable contribution to the growth and development of children and should be considered an integral part of the curriculum. However, for games to be effective teaching tools, they must be played to accomplish specific learning objectives, be developmentally appropriate, and meaningful for children. *The Ultimate Homeschool Physical Education Game Book* contains a variety of games that meet the above criteria and have proven to be very successful with children.

Each game provides everything needed for its successful use, including an introduction with a skill purpose, suggested age category, number of players required, equipment needed, and easy-to-understand play instructions. Also included are helpful illustrations and diagrams to help you visualize the set-up and directions. A user-friendly glossary with important skill and game terminology is located at the beginning of each sport chapter. In the appendix you will find valuable tips for keeping children physically fit, as well as recommended resources for attaining additional information on teaching physical education.

In addition, you will find a chapter devoted to helping you use these game activities most effectively in your homeschool physical education program. This includes how to introduce games to children, finding the right game to help achieve your learning objectives, safety guidelines, and much more.

For over two decades I have searched for new ideas, games, and resource materials to keep children actively involved with games they enjoy playing and which help them develop movement, sport, and fitness skills. This search, coupled with my work with children and parents, has led to this select collection of games. My desire is that *The Ultimate Homeschool Physical Education Game Book* provides you with a valuable tool to make a positive difference in the lifestyles of your children, and to set them on the road to healthy lives.

# CONTENTS

## Section Nine — Fitness-Building Games — 161

## Section Ten — Rope Jumping Activities — 175

"The years of childhood are brief. They should be years filled with wonder and the beautiful magic of play, of growing, of knowing."

*Clare Cherry, author*

# USING GAMES SUCCESSFULLY
# IN PHYSICAL EDUCATION

In general, most games for children represent real-life situations in miniature. Likewise, a physical education game is essentially a learning laboratory where children can apply movement skills in a game-like setting. Contrary to what some may believe, game playing is an important part of the instructional process, and vital to a child's overall physical, emotional, and social development. For home educators to best understand the role of game playing in physical education, let's start by examining the educational value behind their use.

## The Value Of Games In Physical Education

The optimal skill learning experience in physical education starts with teacher instruction, followed by student practice, and culminates in a game-type activity which allows children to develop their newly learned skills. Despite the many positives of game playing in physical education, games should never replace the necessity of teacher instruction and student practice. It's critical to the learning of a newly introduced skill that these steps take place prior to the playing of a game. However, as any educator or parent will tell you, the "game" is what children really look forward to in an instructional setting. They don't want to practice endlessly one specific skill. Formal drills for an extended amount of time require a lot of self-discipline, and few children are sufficiently motivated to do that. Most children want to learn as they play. It's not uncommon to have students develop a more intense interest in practicing their skills once they have participated in games. Enthusiasm and long-term motivation is critical to keeping kids moving, and in the process, enhancing their skill and physical fitness levels.

Based upon his work with homeschooling families, the author has concluded that it is the game stage of the P.E. instructional process causing the home educator the most difficulty. The challenge is finding partner and small group games that are skill-based, developmentally appropriate, fun, and require only minimum equipment. Because of this, the instructional process in the home setting often ends prematurely at the student practice stage. As mentioned, a high level of student interest will be maintained if skills can be practiced through the use of fun and challenging games.

## Achieving Specific Learning Objectives

Aside from the importance of fun and enthusiasm derived from game playing, there are two additional categories of educational benefits. These include *comprehension objectives* and *physical objectives*. Here are some of the specific benefits in each of these groups:

### Comprehension Objectives
- Cultivating a respect for rules and procedures

13

- Learning the value of goals—as well as developing the patience and determination to accomplish those goals
- Developing sportsmanship and an appreciation that one can compete against someone and still be a friend
- Learning game concepts such as offense and defense
- Understanding the value of fairness and honesty
- Developing a cooperative attitude when working with others
- Discovering one's capabilities
- Developing patience and acceptance regarding one's limitations and the limitations of others
- Cultivating readiness skills such as listening, following directions, resolving conflict, solving problems, and thinking strategically
- Enhancing academic skills
- Developing a knowledge of the implications and benefits derived from the participation in fitness-oriented activities

### Physical Objectives

- Improving fundamental movement abilities
- Enhancing sport-specific skills in team and recreational sports
- Developing manipulative skills
- Improving strength, speed, agility, flexibility, and body control
- Enhancing aerobic endurance
- Enhancing the use of spatial awareness skills by learning how to move safely within a group setting
- Developing eye-hand and eye-foot coordination

When choosing games for your physical education lesson, first define the learning objective you want to achieve. Naturally, different games emphasize different skills. Once you have decided on a specific learning objective, look for the game activity that best meets that objective and is developmentally appropriate for your age children. The physical, mental, and emotional levels of your children should also play a part in selecting appropriate games. Readers can find a game's objective in this text by simply looking at the introduction and purpose statement. There you will find what benefit(s) children will gain from the playing of that particular game.

# Maximizing Participation

Maximizing participation to enhance learning is patterned after the inclusive style of teaching. It is based on the principle that every child should be included in the learning process 100 per cent of the time at a level that meets his or her individual needs and abilities. A child cannot benefit from a game unless he is actively involved. In other words, during any specific instructional activity, including games, *no child* is excluded from learning, playing, or participating. Classroom instructors, including home educators, have used this style of teaching for years. Unfortunately, the same can't be said for many physical educators. The use of traditional physical education games that exclude children from the learning process is far too prevalent.

14

To give you an example of how the inclusive style works, let's look at two old standbys *Steal the Bacon* and *Line Soccer*. In a traditional setting with twenty-four children, the instructor would divide the group into two teams and assign each child a number. Following the regular play instructions, only two or four children are going to be active at any given time. The other twenty-something children are standing and waiting. Additionally, because the numbers are called at random, the children may be mismatched in their skill ability or size. In such instances, the disadvantaged children are subject to peer pressure and public ridicule.

*Duck, Duck, Goose* is another popular, but non-inclusive game in which only two players are active at a time, while the rest are sitting and waiting for turns that may never come. Only one child is experiencing success at any given time, and it's usually at the expense of another child. Unfortunately, these types of games are the mainstays of many physical education and youth recreational programs around the country.

What can be done to change games so they become inclusive? First, consider changing and modifying the game rules, boundaries, and strategy. One of the easiest ways this can be done is to place children in pairs and/or small groups, and play several or multiple games simultaneously. Take the partner games listed in this book, *Steal the Bacon* and *Duck, Duck, Goose*. In a large group setting of twenty-four children, there would be 12 games being played simultaneously. There are twenty-four children actively playing 100% of the time. As the parent, teacher, or game leader, you can match up children according to their developmental levels to equalize each child's chance for success. By changing the way a game is played, each child can be included in playing, participating, learning, and experiencing success.

## Guidelines For Teaching Games

Once you have chosen a game that meets your desired instructional objective, it is time to present it to the children. Here are some guidelines to use for teaching games:

1. Know the game well, including the strategy and player objectives, before teaching it.

2. To minimize any wasted instructional time, have the players take positions in a starting position before explaining the rules.

3. Be brief and to the point. Start with just enough rules to get the game started, then add other rules as the situation arises.

4. Present game rules sequentially in small steps. Combine the oral explanation with a demonstration.

5. Remind children of safety considerations associated with the game.

6. Before play is under way, ensure that the children have a sufficient understanding of the rules by allowing a time for questions.

6. While play is under way, provide positive constructive feedback and appropriate encouragement. The feedback should highlight what is good about the child's performance, as well as what can be improved.

7. To prevent confusion, have the players wear identification equipment such as vests, pinnies, flags, or armbands.

8. Stress enjoyment and competition based on "improving," not "proving."

After playing the game, use a question-and-answer session with the children to evaluate if specific learning objectives were met, and if the children understood and enjoyed the game. Use this feedback to determine your next instructional step.

# Safety Considerations

In addition to teaching children the rules and strategy of playing a game, educators need to teach safe play and provide safe playing areas. The following suggestions will help reduce accidents and injuries in your physical education program:

1. Ensure that the play area is free of holes, posts, debris, or other obstacles.

2. Establish boundary lines that are far enough away from walls and fences so children will not run into them.

3. Teach children to stop and start on given signals.

4. Make sure the children have sufficient spatial awareness skills before introducing tag and chasing games in a group setting.

5. Make sure the children are dressed properly. Require athletic shoes and prohibit the wearing of chains, dangling earrings, etc.

6. Provide an adequate warm-up, including stretching exercises, prior to the playing of a game.

7. Model the safe use of any special equipment before the start of a game.

**Special Note**: In an attempt to make the following game directions as brief and concise as possible, the term he and him are used throughout this book to represent both genders equally.

# BASKETBALL GAMES

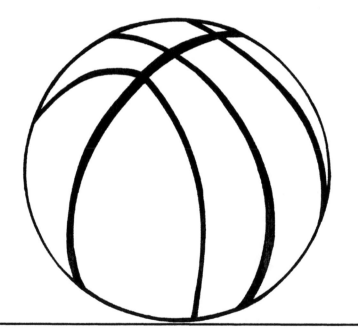

The game of basketball is played by people of all ages in the United States and around the world. One of the many reasons for this is the widespread availability of courts. Besides the local parks, gymnasiums, and school grounds, many families have hoops in their driveways and backyards. The modified basketball games in this section can be played in any indoor or outdoor setting and require few participants–making them perfect for the home schooling family and small group play.

# GLOSSARY OF BASKETBALL TERMS & SKILLS

**ASSIST:** A pass made to a teammate who scores immediately afterwards.

**BACKBOARD:** The flat rectangular or fan-shaped surface attached to the basket.

**BACKCOURT:** The half of the court that is closest to the opponent's goal.

**BASEBALL PASS:** A one-handed, overhand pass that has the same motion as throwing a baseball.

**BASKET:** The name of the cylinder and net at which players shoot the basketball.

**BOUNCE PASS:** A pass that bounces (usually once) on the floor before being caught.

**CENTER:** The name of the offensive player that usually plays closest to the basket. This is often the tallest player on offense.

**CHEST PASS:** A two-handed pass thrown chest level high to a teammate. The pass should be caught at chest level height.

**DEFENSE:** The team not in possession of the ball.

**DOUBLE DRIBBLE:** A dribbling violation in which a player dribbles with two hands.

**DOUBLE TEAM:** Occurs when two players on defense guard one offensive player.

**DRIBBLE:** The bouncing of the ball, with one hand, that allows an offensive player to move around the court.

**DRIVE:** A continuous movement toward the goal by an offensive player.

**FAST BREAK:** Occurs when the offensive team attempts to move the ball down the court as quickly as possibly before the defensive team as a chance to set up.

**FORWARD:** The name of an offensive position. There are usually two forwards on offense.

**FOUL:** A contact violation that results in a loss of ball possession or the awarding of free throw shots.

**FREE THROW:** A shot taken from behind a line called the free throw line. It is an uncontested shot that usually follows a foul violation on the opposing team.

**FRONT COURT:** The name of the half court that is closest to a team's basket.

**GIVE AND GO:** The name of an offensive maneuver in which one player makes a pass and then quickly moves toward the basket for a return pass.

**GUARD:** The name of a position. There are usually two guards playing at one time. These players are responsible for bringing the ball down the court, setting up plays for the center and forwards, etc.

**JUMP BALL:** The event in which the referee puts the ball in play by tossing it up into the air between two opposing players. This is commonly used to start a game.

**LAY-UP:** The name of the shot that bounces off the backboard and into the basket. The shooter attempts this shot on a non-stopping drive toward the basket.

**MAN-TO-MAN DEFENSE:** The name of a type of defensive maneuver in which one defensive player is guarding one offensive player at all times.

**OFFENSE:** The term used to describe the team that has possession of the ball.

**PIVOT:** The name of an action taken by an offensive player with possession of the ball when he rotates on one foot without picking up the other foot. This allows the player to position himself better for a pass or shot attempt.

**PRESS:** The name of a defensive maneuver in which the defensive players are closely guarding the offensive players in both the front and backcourt.

**REBOUND:** A missed shot that bounces off the basket or backboard.

**SCREEN:** The name of an offensive maneuver in which one player (without the ball) positions himself by a defender in order to free up a teammate to receive a pass or take a shot.

**TECHNICAL FOUL:** A violation that usually results from an unsportsmanlike act from a player or coach. The opposing team receives free throw shots and ball possession.

**TRAVELING:** An offensive violation that results from the dribbler taking too many steps with the ball, or starts dribbling again after having stopped the dribble.

**ZONE DEFENSE:** The name of a defensive maneuver in which the defensive players guard only the offensive players that enter into a designated area of the backcourt.

# AROUND THE WORLD

**INTRODUCTION & PURPOSE:** This basketball shooting game has long been an all-time favorite with children. It can be played in any setting as long as one basket is available (the school playground, local park, and family driveway are popular locations).

Shooting skills from a variety of distances and locations around the basket are developed by this activity.

**NUMBER OF PLAYERS:** 2 (additional players can be added)

**SUGGESTED AGE LEVEL:** 8-17 years of age

**EQUIPMENT:** 1 basket, 1 basketball

**HOW TO PLAY:** Designate shooting spots around one basket as shown in the diagram. Players decide a shooting order.

The first shooter attempts two shots from spot #1. If successful, he advances to spot #2. If unsuccessful, the next player shoots from spot #1. As long as a player is successful with one of the two shots, he keeps advancing to the next spot. The objective is to be the first player to make baskets from each of the eight spots, and back again.

**VARIATION:** Allow players the option of either shooting a second shot or beginning their next turn at the spot in which they previously stopped. As a player advances, this strategy becomes more advantageous.

**INTRODUCTION & PURPOSE:** *Basketball Golf* is an exciting combination-sport game that develops the skill of basketball shooting using golf strategies and scorekeeping. It's the perfect alternative, or addition, to the other shooting games described in this section that require the use of only one basket.

**NUMBER OF PLAYERS:** 2 (although up to 4 players can play at one time at each basket)

**SUGGESTED AGE LEVEL:** 9-17 years of age

**EQUIPMENT:** 1 basket, 1 basketball, 3-9 hula hoops (or substitute jump ropes)

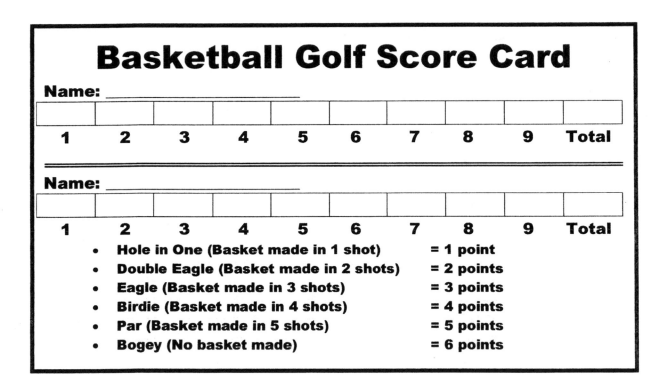

**Basketball Golf Score Card**

Name: _____

| 1 | 2 | 3 | 4 | 5 | 6 | 7 | 8 | 9 | Total |
|---|---|---|---|---|---|---|---|---|---|

Name: _____

| 1 | 2 | 3 | 4 | 5 | 6 | 7 | 8 | 9 | Total |
|---|---|---|---|---|---|---|---|---|---|

- Hole in One (Basket made in 1 shot)    = 1 point
- Double Eagle (Basket made in 2 shots)  = 2 points
- Eagle (Basket made in 3 shots)         = 3 points
- Birdie (Basket made in 4 shots)        = 4 points
- Par (Basket made in 5 shots)           = 5 points
- Bogey (No basket made)                 = 6 points

**HOW TO PLAY:** Randomly place the hula hoops around the court near the basket. Since each hula hoop represents a golf "hole," assign a number to each hula hoop. Players decide a shooting order.

The first shooter attempts to make a shot from hula hoop #1. If he makes it on the first attempt, he receives one point. If he misses, he continues to shoot from that spot, counting one point for each attempt. When the first player is finished, the next player then shoots from the same spot. When each player is done with a "hole," they advance to the next hula hoop. The players keep score as they would in the game of golf. The objective is to have the lowest score possible (which means finishing the course by taking fewer shot attempts than the opponent).

# BASKETBALL
# KING OF THE DRIBBLERS

**INTRODUCTION & PURPOSE:** Children of all ages will enjoy this challenging dribbling game. While *King Of The Dribblers* does not require a basket, a hard or paved surface is needed for ball dribbling.

The skills of dribbling, ball control, and ball stealing are enhanced by this activity.

**NUMBER OF PLAYERS:** 3 (larger groups can play simultaneously on additional play areas)

**SUGGESTED AGE LEVEL:** 8-17 years of age

**EQUIPMENT:** 1 basketball, 1 cone

**HOW TO PLAY:** A playing area approximately 40 feet by 40 feet in size is adequate for most age groups. Place a cone at the end of the playing area. Two players begin behind the cone while the third player stands out in the playing area holding a basketball.

On a starting signal, the player with the ball ("King") begins dribbling while the first player behind the cone gives chase and attempts to steal away the ball using his hands. If successful, the chaser now becomes "King" and takes possession of the ball. The player who lost his ball runs to the back of the cone, and the next player in line runs out and attempts to steal away the King's ball. Play continues in this fashion throughout the game. The objective for each player is to become King and last as long as possible in that position.

It might be useful to set a time limit on the chaser. This prevents the possibility of the player behind the cone waiting for too long.

22

# BASKETBALL PIRATE

**INTRODUCTION & PURPOSE:** The parent/teacher will find this game to be very popular and often requested by children! *Basketball Pirate* does not require a basketball court, although a paved or hard surface is needed for ball dribbling.

The skills of dribbling, ball control, and ball stealing are enhanced by this fun and challenging game.

**NUMBER OF PLAYERS:** 4 (additional players can play with additional pirates added)

**SUGGESTED AGE LEVEL:** 6-12 years of age

**EQUIPMENT:** 1 basketball for each dribbler

**HOW TO PLAY:** Designate one player to start as the Pirate. The Pirate stands without a basketball opposite the other players (dribblers) who are scattered in a playing area that is about 30 feet by 30 feet in size. On a signal, the Pirate chases the dribblers and attempts to steal a basketball. If successful, the Pirate becomes a dribbler, and the player who had his ball stolen becomes the new Pirate. The objective is to last the game without becoming a Pirate.

Dribblers must dribble continuously throughout the game using legal dribbling techniques.

# BASKETBALL
# RED LIGHT – GREEN LIGHT

**INTRODUCTION & PURPOSE:**   This game is a basketball version of the popular children's game Red Light-Green Light. It does not require a basket and it can be played in any setting in which a hard surface exists for dribbling.

　　Dribbling and ball control are the primary basketball skills developed.

**NUMBER OF PLAYERS:**  2-4  (a larger group can play if space permits)

**SUGGESTED AGE LEVEL:**  6-12 years of age

**EQUIPMENT:**  1 basketball for each dribbler

**HOW TO PLAY:**  Mark off two lines that are approximately 40 feet apart. One player begins as the caller while the other players (dribblers) stand on the opposite line, each with a basketball.

　　This game is played much like regular Red Light-Green Light. The caller turns his back to the dribbler and calls out "Green Light!" This is the signal for the dribblers to advance toward the caller by dribbling. On "Red Light!" the caller waits for 3 seconds and turns around. The dribblers must stop dribbling and can't be moving their feet. If a dribbler is caught moving, he must go back to the starting line. The objective of the dribblers is to eventually make it safely to the caller and touch him. The first player to do this becomes the new caller. Play continues in this fashion throughout the game.

24

# BASKETBALL TAG

**INTRODUCTION & PURPOSE:** The rules and strategy of *Basketball Tag* are very similar to the soccer game of *Dribble Freeze Tag* (page 66). The main difference is that players are now dribbling with their hands instead of their feet in this game. No basket is needed, but a hard or paved surface is needed for dribbling.

Dribbling and ball control are the skills developed by this activity.

**NUMBER OF PLAYERS:** 3-4 (larger groups can play with additional taggers)

**SUGGESTED AGE LEVEL:** 6-14 years of age

**EQUIPMENT:** 1 basketball for each dribbler

**HOW TO PLAY:** A playing area approximately 40 feet by 40 feet in size is ideal for most age groups. Designate one player to start as the tagger. The other players (dribblers) stand with a basketball anywhere within the playing area.

On a starting signal, the dribblers move throughout the playing area with the tagger attempting to touch any of the dribblers. A tagged dribbler must stop immediately and sit on his ball. The tagged player can't move unless touched by a dribbler on the shoulder, thereby freeing him to play again. The objective of the dribblers is to avoid getting tagged, while the tagger wants to freeze everyone to stop the game. Play for up to 1-3 minutes, with a new tagger chosen for each game.

Players must use correct dribbling techniques throughout the game.

# BULL IN THE RING

**INTRODUCTION & PURPOSE:** *Bull In The Ring* is similar in strategy to the popular playground game of Keep Away. It doesn't require a basket or court, and it can be played in any outdoor or indoor setting.

Passing, catching, and ball stealing are the primary basketball skills developed in this activity.

**NUMBER OF PLAYERS:** 4 (additional games can be played simultaneously for larger-sized groups)

**SUGGESTED AGE LEVEL:** 8-14 years of age

**EQUIPMENT:** 1 basketball

**HOW TO PLAY:** Start with three players standing in a triangular formation with each player holding a basketball. A fourth player begins as the "Bull" in the middle. On a starting signal, the players pass the ball back and forth while the Bull attempts to touch or intercept a pass. If successful, the Bull switches immediately with the player who last touched the ball. This player becomes the new Bull. The objective is to last the game without becoming a Bull.

To encourage accurate passes, consider implementing a rule that requires a player to become a Bull if he is responsible for an errant pass that exits the triangle.

**INTRODUCTION & PURPOSE:** *Got Ya* is a dribbling game that children of all ages will enjoy and find challenging. One of the benefits of this activity is the emphasis on keeping the eyes up while dribbling. Dribbling and knocking away another player's basketball at the same time is impossible unless this skill is introduced. Also, the chasing and fleeing aspect of this activity provides children with a healthy aerobic conditioning benefit.

**NUMBER OF PLAYERS:** 2-4 (although a higher number can participate if space allows)

**SUGGESTED AGE LEVEL:** 7-17 years of age

**EQUIPMENT:** 1 basketball for each player

**HOW TO PLAY:** Mark off a playing area that is approximately 40 feet by 40 feet in size. Each player starts with a basketball and stands anywhere within the playing area.

On a signal, the players dribble within the playing area while at the same time, trying to knock away other players' basketballs with their free hand. Players yell out "Got Ya" each time they successfully knock away a basketball. A player who loses his basketball can quickly retrieve it and rejoin the game. The objective is to knock away more balls than anyone else.

Encourage the players to use correct dribbling techniques throughout the game.

# FIVE PASSES

**INTRODUCTION & PURPOSE:** The principle objective of this activity is to improve basketball passing skills. Other benefits of *Five Passes* include the development of defensive guarding skills, improved catching and pivoting skills, and increased aerobic endurance.

**NUMBER OF PLAYERS:** 4 players

**SUGGESTED AGE LEVEL:** 8-17 years of age

**EQUIPMENT:** 1 basketball

**HOW TO PLAY:** Use a playing area that is about half a basketball court in size. Designate one team (two players) to start on offense with possession of the ball. The two defensive players stand ready to guard the offensive players.

   The offensive team starts with a pass attempt from the player with the ball to his teammate. The objective is to pass the ball back and forth five consecutive times. However, the defensive players can intercept or knock away all pass attempts. If a defensive player gains possession of the ball, his team immediately becomes the offensive team and they attempt to pass the ball back and forth five consecutive times. The players follow regulation basketball rules in regards to dribbling, fouling, and ball handling. A rule violation results in the other team gaining possession of the ball. The first team to successfully make five consecutive passes wins the game.

   To encourage constant passing and ball movement, consider adding a five second limitation on any player having possession of the ball.

# HORSE

**INTRODUCTION & PURPOSE:** This popular basketball game is a terrific activity for developing a variety of shooting skills. *Horse* is also an ideal instructional choice for the homes setting as it requires only a few participants and the use of one basket.

**NUMBER OF PLAYERS:** 2 (although any number of players can play at one time as long as they take turns in a shooting order)

**SUGGESTED AGE LEVEL:** 9-17 years of age

**EQUIPMENT:** 1 basketball, 1 backboard

**HOW TO PLAY:** The players decide a shooting order. The first player begins the game by taking a shot from any place on the court. If the shot is successful, the second player must also make it from the same spot. If he misses, the letter "H" is given to the player. No letter is given to the player if he makes it. The players alternate in this fashion. The objective is to make a shot and hope that the next player misses, causing the letters HORSE to be spelled against the opposing player. The game ends when one player has HORSE spelled against him.

**VARIATION:** Consider using a shorter or longer animal name such as Cow, Dog, Cat, Rhinoceros, and so forth.

**INTRODUCTION & PURPOSE:** This activity introduces children to the game of basketball without the stress of dribbling. The skill of dribbling, particularly in a competitive setting, is one of the more difficult basketball skills for young children to perform with proficiency. Another advantage of this game is that no single player can "hog" the ball since only passes are used to move the ball around the court.

   With the exception of dribbling, all of the major basketball skills are developed in this activity.

**NUMBER OF PLAYERS:** 2 players on each team (although up to 5 players on a team can play at one time if using a full-size basketball court)

**SUGGESTED AGE LEVEL:** 8-14 years of age

**EQUIPMENT:** 1 basket, 1 basketball

**HOW TO PLAY:** *No Dribble Basketball* is played exactly like *Two-On-Two Basketball* (page 33) with one exception–no dribbling is allowed. Thus, children should have a basic knowledge and proficiency in the skills of pivoting (see glossary) and passing before the introduction of this game.

   A half court size playing area is needed. Two players start with the ball on offense near the out-of-bounds line opposite the basket. The other two players begin on defense. The strategy and rules of this game are similar to regulation basketball with the following exceptions:

1. No dribbling is allowed. A dribbling violation results in a loss of possession.
2. There are no free throw shots after a foul violation. The team with a player fouled throws the ball in at the nearest out of bounds.
3. If the defensive team takes possession of the ball after a missed shot, they must first dribble or pass the ball past the free throw line before scoring.

4. A player has 5 seconds to pass the ball or attempt a shot after stopping his dribble. A violation results in the opponents throwing the ball in at the nearest out of bounds.
5. After each goal, the team scored upon starts with the ball at the out of bounds line opposite the basket.

A team receives two points for each goal made. The objective is to outscore the opponents.

**VARIATION:** Consider playing on a full-size court, especially if additional players are available. The same rules above would still apply. The advantage here would be the addition of different types of passes available for the players to use. Baseball passes, longer cross-court passes, etc., could be better executed on a larger court.

# ONE-ON-ONE BASKETBALL

**INTRODUCTION & PURPOSE:** This terrific learning activity maximizes ball contact opportunities and requires tremendous hustle and concentration. With the exception of passing, *One-On-One Basketball* utilizes and develops all the major skills of basketball.

**NUMBER OF PLAYERS:** 2 players

**SUGGESTED AGE LEVEL:** 9-17 years of age

**EQUIPMENT:** 1 basket, 1 basketball

**HOW TO PLAY:** *One-On-One Basketball* is played using a half-court size playing area. Designate one player to start with the ball on offense at the boundary line opposite the basket. The other player begins on defense. This game is played much like regulation basketball with the same rules that govern dribbling, fouling, and scoring. The exceptions are:
1) There are no free throw shots after a foul violation. The player fouled starts with possession of the ball at the nearest out of bounds.
2) If a missed shot is rebounded by the opponent, the ball must be dribbled past the free throw line before a shot can be made. However, an "air ball" missed shot can be rebounded and a score made immediately without crossing the free throw line.
3) An offensive player who stops his dribble must shoot from that spot.
4) The player scored upon starts each time with the ball at the out of bounds mark opposite the basket.

A player receives two points for each goal. As with regular basketball, the objective is to score more points than the opponent.

# TWO-ON-TWO BASKETBALL

**INTRODUCTION & PURPOSE:** This game is a natural learning progression of *One-On-One Basketball* (opposite page), and can be played in any indoor or outdoor setting as long as one basket is available.

Passing, shooting, dribbling, rebounding, and defensive skills are developed in this activity.

**NUMBER OF PLAYERS:** 4 players (2 players on each team)

**SUGGESTED AGE LEVEL:** 9-17 years of age

**EQUIPMENT:** 1 basket, 1 basketball

**HOW TO PLAY:** A half-court size playing area is needed with one basket. Two players start on offense with the ball near the out of bounds line opposite the basket. The other two players are on defense. The defensive players can decide which offensive player they will guard. This game is played much like regulation basketball with the same rules that govern dribbling, fouling, and scoring. The exceptions are:
   1) There are no free throw shots after a foul violation. The team with a player fouled starts with the ball at the nearest out of bounds.
   2) If the defensive team gains possession of the ball after a missed shot, they must first dribble or pass the ball past the free throw line before scoring.
   3) After each goal, the team scored upon starts with the ball at the out of bounds line opposite the basket.
A team receives two points for each goal. The objective is to score more points than the opponents.

# TRIPLE ACTION
# BASKETBALL

**INTRODUCTION & PURPOSE:** This game is played much like *One-On-One Basketball* (page 32) with the exception that now three players are on the court at one time with each player being a "team."

All of the major basketball skills are enhanced through this activity.

**NUMBER OF PLAYERS:** 3 players

**SUGGESTED AGE LEVEL:** 9-17 years of age

**EQUIPMENT:** 1 basket, 1 basketball

**HOW TO PLAY:** A half-court size playing area is needed with one basket. One player starts with the ball on offense near the free throw line. The other two players begin on defense. The defensive players remain on defense until one of them steals the ball or rebounds a missed shot. This player becomes the new offensive player with the previous offensive player now becoming a defensive player. Anytime an offensive player makes a shot, he receives 2 points and continues as the offensive player by starting with the ball again at the free throw line. If the defensive players force a stopped dribble, the offensive player has three seconds to shoot from that spot.

A dribbling or rule violation on the offensive player results in a jump ball between the two defensive players. In this case, the offensive player tosses the ball between the defensive players at the free throw line. The offensive player cannot gain possession of the jump ball.

The objective for each player is to end the game with more points than the other players.

# KNOCK OUT

**INTRODUCTION & PURPOSE:** This shooting and rebounding game requires one basket and can be played outdoors or in a gymnasium. Because this game is much more competitive and complex in its rules than *Horse* and *Around The World,* it is appropriate for older children.

Besides developing the skill of shooting, *Knock Out* teaches rebounding, hustling, and concentration.

**NUMBER OF PLAYERS:** 3-4 players

**SUGGESTED AGE LEVEL:** 12-17 years of age

**EQUIPMENT:** 1 basket, 1 basketball for each player

**HOW TO PLAY:** The object of this game is to "knock out" the opposing players by making a shot ahead of them. Players begin by standing in a file behind the free throw line. The first shooter attempts to make a shot from the free throw line. If he makes it, he goes to the back of the line and remains in the game. If he misses, he has to quickly rebound the ball and lay it in. As he is doing this, the next player in line shoots from the free throw line. If the shot goes in before the first player makes his follow-up shot, the first player is out of the game. The remaining two players continue playing in this fashion until only one player is left.

# TWENTY-ONE

**INTRODUCTION & PURPOSE:** Because it requires only several players, *Twenty-One* is an ideal shooting game for the family and small group setting. Depending on the age level of the participants, this game can be played a couple of different ways (see the variations below).

Children will find this to be a fun and challenging approach to developing shooting skills.

**NUMBER OF PLAYERS:** 2-4 players

**SUGGESTED AGE LEVEL:** 9-17 years of age

**EQUIPMENT:** 1 basket, 1 basketball

**HOW TO PLAY:** Players decide a shooting order, and stand in a single file behind the free throw line. The first shooter attempts a shot from the free throw line, and a follow-up shot from the spot where the ball is retrieved. A shot made from the free throw line is worth 2 points, and a follow-up shot is worth 1 point. If the player makes both shots, he goes back to the free throw line and continues shooting a long shot and follow-up shot until he misses. A missed shot results in the next player having a chance to shoot from the free throw line.

The objective is to be the first player to reach exactly 21 points. Going over 21 points results in the other player winning the contest. In other words, a player with 20 points would want to deliberately miss a free throw shot but make the follow-up shot worth 1 point.

**VARIATION:** The game would be played exactly as above, except now the opposing player stations himself as a rebounder under the basket. After a missed shot, the rebounder attempts to get possession of the ball and shoots. If the rebounder makes a shot, he receives 1 point and goes to the free throw line for his chance at shooting. If the shooter rebounds the ball and makes the follow-up shot, he receives 1 point and goes back to the free throw line again.

# Section 2

# FOOTBALL GAMES

The game of football is universal in its appeal to children. It seems every child has a favorite team. However, the rules and strategies of football can be overwhelming for children introduced to the sport for the first time. The games in this chapter help teach children the basics of football in a fun and meaningful setting–and yes, there are football-type games that can be played with as few as two players!

# GLOSSARY OF FOOTBALL
# TERMS & SKILLS

**BLOCK:** An action by one of the offensive players to help prevent an opponent from tackling a teammate with the football. This usually entails using the body as a shield.

**COMPLETED PASS:** When an offensive player catches a pass without dropping it or having it intercepted.

**DEFENSIVE TEAM:** The team without possession of the football.

**DEFENSIVE BACK:** A defensive player whose primary responsibility is to guard a receiver running downfield to catch a pass. The defensive back usually attempts to knock a pass away or intercept a pass made to the receiver he is guarding.

**FIELD GOAL:** A score (worth three points) that occurs when the team on offense kicks the football over and between the uprights of the football goal.

**FUMBLE:** An action in which the player with the ball loses control of it, causing it to fall on the ground. Either team can gain possession by recovering it.

**GOAL LINE:** The ends of a rectangular shaped football field. A player with possession of the football wants to cross the opponent's goal line to score a touchdown.

**HANDOFF:** An exchange of the football between two players. This usually entails the quarterback handing the football to another offensive player.

**HIKER:** The player on offense whose primary responsibility is to hike the football to the quarterback. In many of the games described in this book, the hiker is also the receiver and will perform both duties.

**HIKING:** A pass made from between the legs of the hiker to the quarterback.

**INCOMPLETE PASS:** A pass that is not caught by an offensive player. An incomplete pass results in the ball being returned to the original line of scrimmage before the next play begins.

**INTERCEPTION:** A pass intended for an offensive player that is caught by a defender.

**KICKOFF:** A kick using a tee that propels the football down the field to the opponents. A kickoff is performed at the start of the game and at the beginning of the second half. It's also performed after each score during the game.

**LINE OF SCRIMMAGE:** This is an imaginary line that runs from the football to both sides of the field. Whenever the football is placed down for an upcoming play, the line of scrimmage becomes the spot where the football lies. Neither team can cross this line until the offensive team hikes the ball.

**OFFSIDE:** This is a rule violation that occurs when a player from either team prematurely crosses the line of scrimmage before the ball is hiked.

**PUNT:** A kick made from the hands (as opposed to the kick made from the tee) that usually occurs when the offensive team has fourth down and a long distance to score or reach a first down. The punt starts with a player holding the football waist height and arms extended. Two or three steps are usually taken before the player drops the ball so that ball contact is made with the top of the foot.

**QUARTERBACK:** The player on offense whose primary responsibility is to pass the football to a receiver.

**RECEIVER:** The player on offense whose primary responsibility is to catch passes made from the quarterback. In many of the games described in this book, the receiver is also the hiker and will perform both duties.

**RUSHER:** The defensive player whose primary responsibility is to chase and tackle the quarterback.

**SIGNALS:** A combination of words called out by the quarterback which indicates when the ball will be hiked from the hiker (or center). The most common usage is "Ready, Set, Hike."

**TACKLE:** When a defensive player has pulled the flag of an offensive player with possession of the football. This stops play and causes the football to be downed at that spot. A two handed touch can substitute for flag pulling.

**TOUCHDOWN:** A score that occurs when a player with possession of the football crosses the opponent's goal line. A touchdown is worth six points.

# PUNT & PASS RELAY

**INTRODUCTION & PURPOSE:** Two of the best attributes of this game are its simplicity and maximum practice opportunities. Players as young as 6 years of age can enjoy the game's objective which is to throw and punt the football as far as possible.

**NUMBER OF PLAYERS:** 2-4 players (although any number can play if the playing area is large enough to accommodate additional players)

**SUGGESTED AGE LEVEL:** 6-13 years of age

**EQUIPMENT:** 1 football for each player

**HOW TO PLAY:** This game is best played on a large field, preferably a football-size field. The goal lines are the starting and finishing lines. Each player begins with a football on the goal line designated as the starting line.

On a signal, each player either punts or throws the ball down the field as far as possible. The players then move up to the spot where their ball has stopped. On the next signal, each player again punts or throws his ball as far as possible toward the finish line, and then moves up to that spot. Play continues in this fashion until each player has successfully crossed the finish line. The objective is to be the first player to cross the finish line.

**VARIATIONS:** To have the game last longer, consider having the players cross one goal line and then work back toward the opposite goal line (in other words, the starting and finishing line would be the same).

# FIRST FOR FIVE

**INTRODUCTION & PURPOSE:** In many ways, *First For Five* resembles a football version of Keep Away (a popular playground game). The football skills of passing, catching, and pass defense are all enhanced in this highly active contest.

**NUMBER OF PLAYERS:** 4 players (although larger groups of up to 8 players can be divided into two teams)

**SUGGESTED AGE LEVEL:** 8-14 years of age

**EQUIPMENT:** 1 football, cone markers (or similar objects to mark off a playing area)

**HOW TO PLAY:** Mark off a square shaped playing area that is approximately 50 feet by 50 feet in size. Form two teams of two players each, and designate one team to start with the football. Each player is assigned to guard a player on the opposite team.

The player with the football begins by passing it to his teammate. The objective is to make five consecutive completed passes. This results in one point being awarded to the team that successfully does this throughout the game. The team at the end of play with the highest number of points wins the contest.

The passer cannot take more than three steps before throwing the ball, and has only 5 seconds in which to throw the ball. Pivoting (as in basketball) is allowed. The ball is awarded to the opposing team if a passer "travels," or takes too long to throw.

The defenders can knock down or intercept any pass attempt. However, defenders cannot touch the passer or the receiver. A touching or rough play violation results in the opponents gaining possession of the ball.

41

# FAKE & SHAKE

**INTRODUCTION & PURPOSE:** In the sport of football, a receiver is constantly faking and running from a defensive player in order to receive a pass from the quarterback (otherwise, the pass can be knocked down or intercepted). This is a wonderful activity for reinforcing the concept of "shaking" a defender.

Fake & Shake also enhances the skills of passing, catching, and defensive guarding.

**NUMBER OF PLAYERS:** 2-3 players on each team (larger groups can play several games simultaneously on different fields)

**SUGGESTED AGE LEVEL:** 9-17 years of age

**EQUIPMENT:** 1 football, cone markers (or similar objects to mark the field boundaries)

**HOW TO PLAY:** Mark off a playing area that is about 30 feet by 50 feet in size with a line down the middle to divide the playing area into two halves. One player from Team A (see diagram above) stands on one side with the football while his teammate stands on the opposite half. Team B also has a player on each side.

The game begins with the player holding the football throwing it to his teammate in the opposite half. A completed pass results in one point for that team. The defensive players (the team without possession of the ball) attempt to stop the pass from being completed by guarding the two offensive players closely. The defensive player guarding the thrower can knock down a pass but cannot make bodily contact. Likewise, the defender guarding the receiver can knock down or intercept a pass but can not touch the receiver. The team with possession of the football maintains possession as long as the ball is not intercepted or retrieved after an incomplete pass by the opposite team.

42

Players can run anywhere on their side of the field. However, they cannot cross the middle line that separates the field into two halves.

Before playing, emphasize the concept that a receiver needs to run and fake the defender in order to be in a position to receive a pass–otherwise, the pass will be knocked down or intercepted. At the same time, the defensive player guarding the receiver needs to understand the necessity of staying close to the receiver in order to prevent a completion.

If keeping score, one point is awarded to the team that makes a successful pass completion. The objective is to have the highest number of points at the conclusion of play.

# FOUR DOWNS

**INTRODUCTION & PURPOSE:** This game introduces the concept of an offensive team having four downs to achieve a score (a touchdown or field goal) or reach a "first down" (which results in another set of four downs).

The skills of passing, catching, hiking, fleeing, and pass defense are all enhanced by this activity.

**NUMBER OF PLAYERS:** 2 players on each team (up to 4 players on a team can be permitted if the playing area is large enough)

**SUGGESTED AGE LEVEL:** 9-17 years of age

**EQUIPMENT:** 1 football, football flags for each player (or substitute handkerchiefs), cone markers, or similar objects, to mark off boundary lines

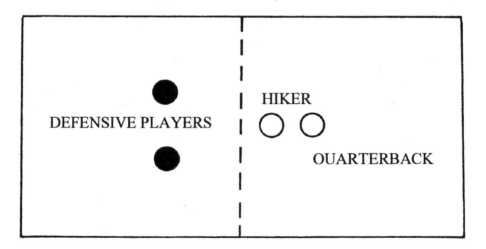

**HOW TO PLAY:** Mark off a rectangular-shaped field approximately 45 feet by 90 feet in size (older players might enjoy a larger sized field). Before starting, all players should have a flag inserted in the back of their waistband for pulling.

Two players start with the ball on their designated goal line. One player is the quarterback and the other is the hiker/receiver. The two defensive players can either both guard the hiker/receiver when he runs downfield to receive a pass, or one defender can guard the hiker/receiver while the other defender rushes the quarterback. The defender rushing the quarterback must first count out loud to 10 or any combination of numbers or words before crossing the line of scrimmage.

The offensive team has four downs to score a touchdown. A touchdown is scored when the hiker/receiver catches a pass and runs past the opponent's goal line without having his flag pulled. An offensive team can also be awarded a "first down" if they complete four straight passes without scoring. In this case, they receive four additional downs with the ball.

There are no kick-offs after a team has scored a touchdown. The non-scoring team simply takes possession of the ball on the opposite goal line with four downs to score or reach a first down.

A team on offense must observe the following rules:  1) The quarterback can not run past the line of scrimmage (even when rushed by a defender). 2) Only forward passes are allowed. 3) There are no hand-offs. A violation of any of these rules results in a loss of down.

The hiker/receiver is "tackled" when his flag is pulled by one of the defensive players (however, he can only be tackled if he has caught a pass and is running with the ball). The ball is put down at the spot of the tackle and the next play begins. An incomplete pass results in the ball remaining at the same spot for the next play.

On fourth down, the offensive team must pass the ball. No punting is allowed. If the fourth down pass is incomplete, the opposing team then takes possession of the ball at their goal line. They now have four downs to score or reach a first down.

A touchdown is worth 6 points. The objective is to end the contest with the highest number of points.

**VARIATION:** For tackling, a two-hand touch can substitute for football flags.

# 49'ER FOOTBALL

**INTRODUCTION & PURPOSE:** Strategically speaking, *49'er Football* is a football version of the basketball game called *Twenty-One* (page 36). However, in this case the team objective is to score exactly 49 points.

In addition to being a terrific mathematical learning activity, this game also develops the football skills of passing, catching, hiking, and pass defense.

**NUMBER OF PLAYERS:** 2 players on each team (larger groups can play simultaneously on separate playing areas)

**SUGGESTED AGE LEVEL:** 9-14 years of age

**EQUIPMENT:** 1 football, cone markers or similar objects to mark a playing area

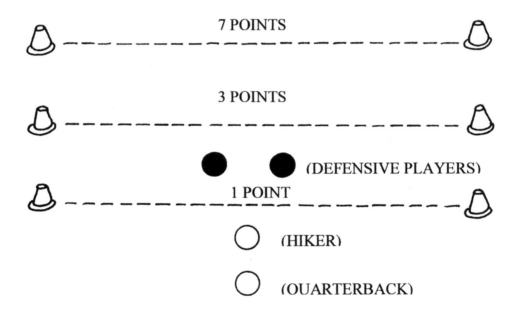

**HOW TO PLAY:** Mark off a playing area as shown in the diagram above, with the cones about 15 feet apart (the older players can make the scoring zones further apart).

One team is designated to start on offense with the ball on the goal line. The offensive team consists of a quarterback and a player (hiker/receiver) who both hikes the ball to the quarterback and attempts to receive a pass thrown from the quarterback. The defensive team can have both players guard the hiker/receiver, or one player can guard while the other player rushes the quarterback. A defender who rushes the quarterback must first count out loud to ten or any combination of numbers or words before crossing the line of scrimmage.

The objective is to be the first team to score exactly 49 points. Points are scored each time a pass is completed. The number of points awarded depends on the spot (scoring zone) where a catch took place. An incomplete pass is not worth any points. Each team has only one play on offense and must switch places with the other team after each play.

# FOOTBALL 100

**INTRODUCTION & PURPOSE:** *Football 100* develops four major football skills–passing, catching, hiking, and pass defense. The emphasis on these particular skills makes it a terrific lead-up experience to regulation flag or touch football.

Game leaders need to ensure that the proper techniques of throwing, catching, hiking and playing defense have been taught and practiced before the introduction of this game.

**NUMBER OF PLAYERS:** 4 players (however, only 3 players are required if you eliminate the receiver position and have the hiker run the pass route after hiking the ball)

**SUGGESTED AGE LEVEL:** 8-17 years of age

**EQUIPMENT:** 1 football

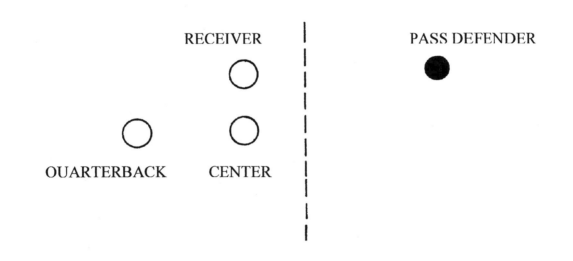

**HOW TO PLAY:** The four players start by assuming a starting position as either the quarterback, center, receiver, or defender (see diagram above). The receiver lines up next to the center in a three-point stance, the defender lines up facing the receiver, and the center begins the game with the football.

The quarterback begins by yelling out "ready, set, hike." On "hike," the center hikes the ball to the quarterback and the receiver runs downfield to catch a pass. The defender should stay as close as possible to the receiver trying to prevent a completed pass. The receiver is awarded 10 points if the pass is caught. However, if the defender catches the pass (an "interception"), he is awarded the 10 points. An incomplete pass is not worth any points. The objective is to be the first player to score 100 points.

Players rotate positions after each play. The quarterback moves to receiver, the receiver to defender, the defender to center, and the center becomes the next quarterback.

# ONE-ON-ONE
# FLAG FOOTBALL

**INTRODUCTION & PURPOSE:** This modified flag football game requires only two participants, can be played in the convenience of a backyard, and has rules so simple that even the youngest of school-age children will enjoy playing.

   The skills developed in this activity include kicking, catching, fleeing, and tackling (pulling the flag).

**NUMBER OF PLAYERS:** 2 players (larger groups can play several games simultaneously)

**SUGGESTED AGE LEVEL:** 6-13 year olds

**EQUIPMENT:** 1 football, 1 kicking tee, 4 cones (or similar objects) for field markers, 2 football flags (or a similar substitute such as handkerchiefs)

**HOW TO PLAY:** Mark off a rectangular field that is about 30 feet by 60 feet in size. The lines at the two ends of the rectangle represent the goal lines. A player starts at each goal line with a flag tucked in the back of his belt (it should be hanging down and easy to pull). One of the two players is designated to kick off first and the other starts as the receiver. A kicking tee and ball should be placed on the goal line.

   The kicker begins the game by kicking the football toward the receiver. The objective of the receiving player is to catch and run with the ball past the opposite goal line without having his flag pulled by the kicking player. If successful, a touchdown (worth six points) is scored for the receiver. No points are awarded if the player's flag is pulled. The players switch roles after each play.

48

If keeping score, the player with the most touchdowns at the end of a designated time period wins the contest.

**VARIATIONS:** Instead of kicking, players can punt when performing the kick-off. For tackling, a two-hand touch can substitute for flag pulling.

Also consider adding two additional players (making for a total of two players on each team) and adding an additional football. This results in two footballs being kicked and returned on each play. In this case, the team returning a kick off would not have a blocker since both players would be carrying a football.

# TRIPLE ACTION FOOTBALL

**INTRODUCTION & PURPOSE:** *Triple Action Football* solves the problem of not having an even number of players to play a football game. This unique game requires exactly three players and is a natural learning progression from *One-On-One Football* (see previous game).

   The skills of throwing, catching, fleeing, kicking, hiking, and tackling (that is, flag pulling or a two-hand touch) are all enhanced in this terrific learning activity.

**NUMBER OF PLAYERS:**  3 players (larger groups can play multiple games simultaneously)

**SUGGESTED AGE LEVEL:**  8-14 years of age

**EQUIPMENT:**  1 football, 1 kicking tee, 4 cones or similar objects for field markers, 3 football flags (or a similar substitute such as handkerchiefs)

**HOW TO PLAY:**  Mark off a rectangular-shaped field that is about 30 feet by 60 feet in size. The two lines at the ends of the rectangle represent the goal lines.

   All three players are to choose a kicking order before starting play. Two players (offensive players) start at one goal while the other player (kicker) stands at the opposite goal line with the tee. Each player is to wear a football flag in the back of their waistband that is hanging and easy to pull.

   The kicker begins the game by kicking off toward the two offensive players. One of the offensive players catches or retrieves the ball and attempts to run it back across the kicker's goal line for a touchdown. The other offensive player blocks for the runner and tries to prevent the kicker from pulling the runner's flag. If the runner scores a touchdown, the next player designated to kick becomes the kicker, the players rotate positions, and the game continues with a kickoff. However, if the runner's flag is pulled before crossing the goal line, then the two offensive players are allowed to try one play from the spot where the runner was "tackled." The formation for each play consists of one offensive player playing quarterback (thrower), one offensive player as the hiker/receiver, and the kicker plays defense by guarding the hiker/receiver. Both offensive players are awarded a touchdown if they successfully score. No points are awarded if the defensive player stops the play. After each play, the players rotate positions with the next designated player becoming the kicker for the next kickoff.

Players are awarded 6 points for scoring a touchdown. Players keep track of their own score.

**VARIATION:** For tackling, a two-hand touch can substitute for flag pulling.

# TWO-ON-TWO FLAG FOOTBALL

**INTRODUCTION & PUROPSE:** *Two-On-Two Flag Football* is a natural learning extension of *One-On-One Flag Football* (page 48). Offensive plays are implemented and the subsequent strategy becomes a significant part of this learning activity.

Kicking, catching, hiking, fleeing, passing, and defensive play are skills developed through this activity.

**NUMBER OF PLAYERS:** 4 players (larger groups can play several games simultaneously)

**SUGGESTED AGE LEVEL:** 8-14 years of age

**EQUIPMENT:** 1 football, 1 kicking tee, 4 cone markers or similar objects to mark a field, 4 football flags (or a similar substitute such as handkerchiefs)

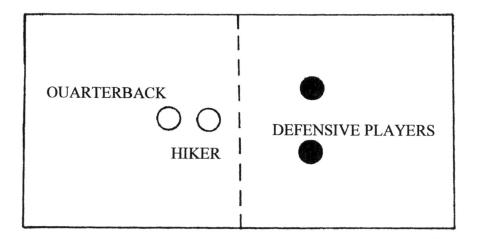

**HOW TO PLAY:** Mark off a rectangular-shaped field that is about 40 feet by 80 feet in size. This can be larger or smaller depending on the age and/or skill level of the players. The lines at the ends of the rectangle represent the goal lines. The offensive team stands near one goal line while the defensive team (kicking team) is positioned on the opposite goal line with a tee. Before starting, all players should have a football flag hanging from the back of their waistband.

The kicking team begins by kicking the ball to the offensive team. One of the offensive players catches or retrieves the ball and attempts to run it past the opponent's goal line for a touchdown. The other offensive player blocks for the runner and tries to prevent the opponents from pulling his flag. If the runner scores, the scoring team then kicks off to the team that was scored upon. If the runner is tackled, the ball is put down at that spot and that team now has one play to score. One offensive player becomes the quarterback and the other player is positioned as the hiker/receiver. The defensive team can either have both players guard the hiker/receiver when he runs downfield for a pass, or one defender can guard while the other defender rushes the quarterback. The rusher must first count out loud to 10 (or any combination of numbers or words) before chasing the quarterback. After the play, regardless of whether the offensive team scores or not, the teams reverse roles and continue play with a new kick-off.

Teams are awarded 6 points for each touchdown. The objective is to end play with more points than the opponents.

**VARIATION:** For tackling, a two-handed touch can substitute for flag pulling.

# ULTIMATE FOOTBALL

**INTRODUCTION & PURPOSE:** *Ultimate Football* is a fast-action game that is especially popular with older children. It is played exactly like *Ultimate* (page 160) with the exception that a football is used exclusively.

Catching, passing, and defensive play are the principle skills developed in this exciting learning activity.

**NUMBER OF PLAYERS:** 2 players on each team (larger-sized groups can play separate games simultaneously)

**SUGGESTED AGE LEVEL:** 10-17 years of age

**EQUIPMENT:** 1 football, cone markers (or similar substitutes to mark the playing area)

**HOW TO PLAY:** Mark off a rectangular shaped playing area that is approximately 60 feet by 120 feet (although this can be smaller or larger depending on the age of the players and available space). The long ends represent the goal lines.

Divide the players into two teams of two players each. Each player is assigned to guard a member of the opposite team. Designate one player to start with the football on his goal line.

As with the game *Ultimate,* the team objective is to have a player catch a pass past the opponent's goal line. The player with the football starts the game by passing to his teammate. Since players with possession of the football can not run with it, the ball is advanced down the field by a combination of completed passes between the two players. Upon catching a pass, a player has only a couple of steps in which to stop. Passers also have only 5 seconds to throw the ball. The opposing team is awarded the football if a player takes too many steps and/or

54

takes too long to throw. As long as a team successfully catches the football, they have an unlimited number of plays to score. Any thrown ball that touches the ground (an incomplete pass) is awarded to the other team at that spot.

Defenders (players without possession of the football) cannot get any closer than three feet to the passer or the receiver. However, a thrown ball can be intercepted which results in the intercepting team gaining possession of the ball at that spot. That team now attempts to score by advancing the ball toward the opposite goal line.

A touchdown (worth 6 points) is awarded each time a player successfully catches a football past the opponent's goal line.

**VARIATION:** Consider eliminating the no traveling rule. Players can run with the football until tackled (flag pulling or a two handed touch). When tackled, a player then has to stay in that spot and has only five seconds to throw the football. This variation will result in more aerobic action and more touchdowns.

# FIELD GOALS GALORE

**INTRODUCTION & PURPOSE:** The skill of kicking is very important in the game of football. Besides extra points and field goals, there are kickoffs to start each half of a game and after each score.

In addition to developing kicking skills, *Field Goals Galore* provides a lot of healthy movement as the players run back and forth between kicking and retrieving the ball.

**NUMBER OF PLAYERS:** 2 players (larger groups can play multiple games simultaneously)

**SUGGESTED AGE LEVEL:** 8-17 years of age

**EQUIPMENT:** 1 football, 1 kicking tee

**HOW TO PLAY:** This game is best played outdoors with access to a football goal or a soccer goal (in this case, the objective would be to kick the ball over the top of the soccer goal post). One player places the tee with the football resting on it about 30 feet away from the goal post (this can vary depending on the age of the players). The other player stands behind the goal post ready to retrieve the kicked ball.

To begin, the kicker runs forward and attempts to kick the ball through the uprights. A ball that goes through the uprights and over the post results in a score of 3 points. The player behind the goal post is to retrieve the ball, run to the tee, set the ball on the tee, and kick in the same manner. The previous kicker now becomes the retriever. The two players continue the same rotation throughout the game.

If keeping score, play for a specified time limit with the player scoring the highest number of points declared the winner. A scoring alternative would be to add the points together and challenge the players to reach a higher collective point total with each contest.

# Section 3

# SOCCER GAMES

Of all the team sports, soccer contains the highest number of physical benefits for children. In addition to being an excellent aerobic activity, soccer is relatively inexpensive to play (a ball and field is all that is needed), and the simple rules and strategies make it the easiest of all the major sports for children to understand.

The games in this section concentrate on developing the major soccer skills (dribbling, passing, trapping, and goalie play) children need to possess in order to enjoy this terrific sport.

# GLOSSARY OF SOCCER
# TERMS & SKILLS

**CORNER KICK:** A place kick made from the corner of the field. This occurs when the defensive team sends the ball out of bounds past the end line or over the top of the goal.

**DIRECT FREE KICK:** A free kick in which a goal can be made directly. The ball is placed where the rule violation occurred.

**DRIBBLING:** The skill of advancing the ball with short taps or pushes with the feet.

**DROPPED BALL:** The action taken by the referee to put the ball into play after a no-penalty situation. The ball is dropped between two players.

**FREE KICK:** A free place kick is awarded to the non-penalized team at the spot where a rule violation occurred. It is labeled either a direct free kick (after a serious violation such as a personal foul) or an indirect free kick (a minor violation such as hands, goalie taking too many steps, etc).

**FOUL:** A rule violation that results in a free kick. Examples of foul violations include: unsportsmanlike conduct, hands, tripping, personal foul, kicking an opponent, goalie taking too many steps, etc.

**GOAL KICK:** A kick made by the defensive team from the goal area after the ball has gone out of bounds past the end line and was touched by an offensive team player.

**GOALKEEPER or GOALIE:** The name of the player who guards the goal. This is the only player allowed to use hands to catch and throw the ball.

**HANDS:** A violation that occurs when a player other than the goalie touches the ball with any part of the arm from the shoulders to the fingers.

**HEADING:** The technique of hitting the ball with the head. This is done by contacting the ball with the forehead around the hairline.

**INDIRECT FREE KICK:** A place kick that must be touched by another player before a goal can be scored. It is awarded to the non-penalized team after a minor rule violation.

**KICK-OFF:** An indirect free kick used to start play at the beginning of the game, at the beginning of the second half, and after each score. The kick is made from the center circle.

**OFFSIDE:** A violation that occurs when a player is nearer to the opponent's goal than the ball. The penalty is loss of ball possession. There are three exceptions for which offsides is not called: 1) the player was the last one to kick the ball; 2) the player is in his own half of the field; 3) two or more opposing players are closer to the goal than he is.

**PENALTY KICK:** A kick by an offensive team player from the penalty kick mark that is 12 yards from the goal. This kick is awarded after the defensive commits a foul within the penalty area. Only the player kicking and the goalkeeper are involved.

**PUNTING:** A type of kick used by the goalkeeper. The ball is dropped from the hands and contacted with a foot before it hits the ground.

**SHOOTING:** Attempting to kick or head the ball into the goal to score a point.

**STRIKER:** The central forward player on the team. This player's main responsibility is to score goals.

**SWEEPER:** The name of the player who positions himself in front of or behind the defender's line. This player's main responsibility is to go after loose passes.

**TACKLE:** The technique of stealing the ball away from an opponent.

**THROW-IN:** A two-handed overhead pass made from the point where the ball has gone out of bounds. The team not responsible for last touching it is awarded the throw-in.

**TRAPPING:** The technique of stopping a ball. Any body part can be used with the exception of the hands and arms.

**WALL:** A group of players who stand in front of the goal to stop a free kick from going in. Players stand at least 10 yards from the point of the kick.

# SOCCER PIRATE

**INTRODUCTION & PURPOSE:** *Soccer Pirate* has the dual benefit of developing the skill of soccer dribbling and enhancing cardiovascular fitness. This non-stop activity is a great example of how the physical fitness objective can also be achieved through a sport skill-building game.

**NUMBER OF PLAYERS:** 3-4 players (larger groups can play with additional taggers)

**SUGGESTED AGE LEVEL:** 6-14 years of age

**EQUIPMENT:** 1 soccer ball for each dribbler

**HOW TO PLAY:** A playing area that is limited to approximately 40 feet by 40 feet is ideal for 3-4 players. Designate one player to start as the Pirate. The other players (dribblers) stand with a foot on top of their ball.

On a starting signal, the dribblers move around the playing area with the Pirate in pursuit. The Pirate attempts to steal a ball from one of the dribblers using only his feet. If successful, the Pirate becomes a dribbler and the player who had his ball stolen becomes the next Pirate. The objective is to avoid becoming a Pirate.

# SOCCER TUNNEL TAG

**INTRODUCTION & PURPOSE:** Children will find this game to be an exciting mix of soccer and tag. Dribbling and ball control are the principle skills developed in this activity.

**NUMBER OF PLAYERS:** 3-4 players (larger-sized groups can play with additional taggers)

**SUGGESTED AGE LEVEL:** 6-13 years of age

**EQUIPMENT:** 1 soccer ball for each player

**HOW TO PLAY:** With 3-4 total players, it would be best to confine the players to a playing area that is approximately 40 feet by 40 feet. Designated one player to start as the tagger. The tagger stands at one end of the playing area holding a soccer ball, while the other players stand at the opposite end with a foot on top of their ball.

On a starting signal, the dribblers move throughout the playing area with the tagger giving chase. The tagger attempts to throw and hit their soccer ball. If a dribbler has his ball hit, he must freeze in a straddle position with his ball held above his head. A tagged player is free when a dribbler kicks a soccer ball between his legs. Play for 1-3 minutes and choose a new tagger each time.

**VARIATION:** Have the tagged player become the new tagger instead of freezing in a straddle position. The game becomes non-stop with no resting (resulting in a great fitness building activity!).

# SOCCER
# RED LIGHT – GREEN LIGHT

**INTRODUCTION & PURPOSE:** Since most children love to play the game of Red Light-Green Light, this modified soccer version of the game is sure to become a favorite as well. The soccer skills of dribbling and ball control take the place of running.

**NUMBER OF PLAYERS:** 2-4 players (although a higher number of players can play at one time if space permits)

**SUGGESTED AGE LEVEL:** 6-12 years of age

**EQUIPMENT:** 1 soccer ball for each dribbler

**HOW TO PLAY:** Mark off two lines that are approximately 40 feet apart. Each dribbler stands on one line with a soccer ball facing the caller (who stands on the opposite line).

This game is played much like regular Red Light- Green Light. The caller turns his back to the dribbler and calls out "Green Light." This is the signal for the dribbler to advance toward the caller. On "Red Light," the caller waits for 3 seconds and turns around. The dribbler must stop dribbling with a foot on top of the ball before the caller turns around. If the dribbler is caught moving, he goes back to the starting line. The objective of the dribbler is to eventually make it safely to the caller where he can tag him. When successful, the players switch roles.

# CRAB SOCCER

**INTRODUCTION & PURPOSE:** *Crab Soccer* is essentially one-on-one soccer with the players moving in a crab position rather than being upright. The players still kick, dribble, play defense, etc. An added bonus to this game is the upper body exercise the children receive as a result of moving in a crab position.

**NUMBER OF PLAYERS:** 2 players (play multiple games simultaneously for larger-sized groups)

**SUGGESTED AGE LEVEL:** 6- 13 years of age

**EQUIPMENT:** 1 soccer ball, 4 cones (or similar objects to mark off goals)

**HOW TO PLAY:** Two cones are placed approximately 10 feet apart at each end to represent the goals. The length of the playing area should be approximately 30-40 feet apart. There are no boundary lines.

The game is played much like *One-On-One Soccer* (see page 72) except the players are now moving in a crab position. One player begins by kicking off in the middle. The objective is to advance the ball toward the opponent's goal and score by kicking the ball between the cones. The defensive player can steal the ball at any time. After each score, a kick off occurs in the middle of the playing area.

Since there are no boundary lines, a player can move the ball in any direction. However, a score can be made only by kicking the ball from inside the playing area.

As with regular soccer, no touching of the ball with the hands is allowed. A violation results in the other player gaining possession of the ball.

**VARIATION:** Consider playing with two players on a team. The same rules above would apply. Both players would be involved in playing offense and defense (no goalies).

# TARGET SOCCER

**INTRODUCTION & PURPOSE:** The simple but challenging rules of *Target Soccer* will appeal to children of all ages. The principle skills developed in this activity include kicking accuracy and trapping.

**NUMBER OF PLAYERS:** 2-4 players (larger groups can play with additional targets in the middle)

**SUGGESTED AGE LEVEL:** 6-17 years of age

**EQUIPMENT:** 2 soccer balls for each pair of players; 1 bowling pin (or similar object) for each pair of players

**HOW TO PLAY:** Mark off two lines that are approximately 30 feet apart. Place a bowling pin (or any substitute such as a cone, playground ball, etc.) in the middle. The players start on opposite lines facing each other, each with a soccer ball.

On a starting signal, the players attempt to kick and hit the bowling pin. The players must stay behind their restraining line when kicking. Play continues for a designated time limit with the player hitting the pin the most often declared the winner.

The game leader retrieves any balls that come to a stop in the middle and equally distributes them to the two players. The game leader also sets up any pin that is knocked down during the contest. In the event there is no game leader, the players can run and retrieve any ball that stops in the middle area. However, kicks have to be attempted from behind the restraining lines.

# SOCCER
# KING OF THE DRIBBLERS

**INTRODUCTION & PURPOSE:** *Soccer King Of The Dribblers* is perfect for the instructional setting that requires three players and has a learning objective of developing soccer dribbling and ball control skills.

**NUMBER OF PLAYERS:** 3 players (larger groups can play simultaneously on additional playing areas)

**SUGGESTED AGE LEVEL:** 7-17 years of age

**EQUIPMENT:** 1 soccer ball, 1 cone (or any object to mark a waiting line)

**HOW TO PLAY:** A playing area of approximately 40 feet by 40 feet in size is adequate for most age groups. Place a cone at one end of the playing area. Two players begin behind the cone while a third player stands in the playing area with a foot on top of the ball.

On a starting signal, the player with the ball begins dribbling while the first player behind the cone gives chase. The chasing player attempts to steal away the ball using his feet. If successful, the chaser now becomes "King" and takes possession of the ball. The player who lost his ball runs to the back of the cone, and the next player in line runs out and attempts to steal away the King's ball. Play continues in this fashion throughout the game. The objective of each player is to become "King" and last as long as possible in that position.

It might be useful to set a time limit on the chaser trying to steal the ball. This would prevent a situation in which one player waits behind the cone for too long of a period.

# DRIBBLE FREEZE TAG

**INTRODUCTION & PURPOSE:**  Children will love this mix of soccer dribbling and tag. In fact, *Dribble Freeze Tag* is essentially the regular game of tag with dribbling replacing the normal movement of running. The simplicity of the rules makes it an ideal game experience for the younger player.

**NUMBER OF PLAYERS:**  3-4 players (larger groups can play with additional taggers)

**SUGGESTED AGE LEVEL:**  6-12 years of age

**EQUIPMENT:**  1 soccer ball for each dribbler

**HOW TO PLAY:**  A playing area that is approximately 40 feet by 40 feet in size is ideal for 3-4 players. One player is designated to start as the tagger. The other players (dribblers) stand scattered throughout the playing area with a foot on top of their ball.

On a starting signal, the dribblers move throughout the playing area with the tagger in pursuit attempting to touch a dribbler. A tagged dribbler must stop immediately and sit on their ball. The tagged player cannot move until he's touched on the shoulder by a dribbler. The objective for the dribblers is to avoid getting tagged, while the tagger wants to freeze everyone to stop the game.

Play for up to 1-3 minutes, with a new tagger chosen for each game.

# SOCCER CRAB TAG

**INTRODUCTION & PURPOSE:** This challenging game is sure to become a favorite with your children. It requires very little space and is easy to play. Besides being an excellent game for developing soccer dribbling, *Soccer Crab Tag* also builds upper body strength because of the required crab position that players are in when not dribbling.

**NUMBER OF PLAYERS:** 3 or more players

**SUGGESTED AGE LEVEL:** 7-17 years of age

**EQUIPMENT:** 1 soccer ball for each player

**HOW TO PLAY:** Mark off a playing circle that is about 15 feet in diameter for a group of 3-4 players. A larger group will need a larger-sized circle. If playing inside a gymnasium, the circles around the free throw lines and mid-court areas will work. Select one player to start inside the circle in a crab position ("It"). The other players stand anywhere inside the circle with a foot on top of their soccer ball.

The object is to last the game as long as possible before being "tagged" by a crab. The game begins with the "It" (the player in the crab position) chasing after the dribbling players and attempting to kick away their soccer balls. If the "It" kicks a dribbler's ball so it exits the circle, that player is "tagged," and becomes a helper of the "It." The helpers immediately assume a crab position and chase after any remaining dribblers. Any dribbler who accidentally kicks his ball outside the circle is tagged regardless of whether an "It" touched the ball. Play stops when only one dribbler remains in the game. The "Its" can only move around in a crab position, are to use only their feet (no hands) to knock away balls, and are not to kick or trip the dribblers. After each contest, choose a new "It" and start play again.

# SOCCER
# STEAL THE BACON

**INTRODUCTION & PURPOSE:** Children will love the challenging aspect of this dribbling and ball control game. In fact, the author's children rank this as one of their very favorites!

**NUMBER OF PLAYERS:** 4 players (3 players can play in the variation described below; larger groups can play games simultaneously on individually marked off playing areas)

**SUGGESTED AGE LEVEL:** 6-17 years of age

**EQUIPMENT:** 5 hula hoops (or jump ropes laid in a circular shape), 4 soccer balls

**HOW TO PLAY:** Place four hula hoops in a square-shaped formation approximately 30 feet apart. One hula hoop is placed in the middle with four soccer balls. Each of the four players stand inside a hula hoop.

On a starting signal, all four players run toward the middle hula hoop, take one soccer ball (with their feet), and dribble the ball back to their hula hoop. After that, each player attempts to steal a ball from another hula hoop while guarding his own ball. The game objective is to be the first player to have two soccer balls inside a hula hoop.

If playing inside a gymnasium, consider using floor tape for circles. This will prevent players from sliding on the hula hoops and injuring themselves.

**VARIATION:** For 3 players, set up a triangular shaped playing area. Same rules would apply as described above.

# SOCCER HORSE

**INTRODUCTION & PURPOSE:** This game is much like *Basketball Horse* (page 29) in its strategy, except now players are kicking goals instead of shooting baskets.

The soccer skills developed in this activity include kicking and goalie play.

**NUMBER OF PLAYERS:** 2 players (mark off additional playing areas for larger groups)

**SUGGESTED AGE LEVEL:** 6-17 years of age

**EQUIPMENT:** 1 soccer ball, 1 soccer goal (or substitute 2 cone markers for a soccer goal)

**HOW TO PLAY:** Set two cone markers approximately 8 feet to 20 feet apart as a soccer goal. One player is designated as the goalie while the other player starts as the kicker.

Each player takes a turn kicking with the objective of scoring a goal (by kicking the ball past the goalie). The kicker can attempt a score from any spot. The goalie tries to stop any score by catching or knocking away the kicked ball. If a score is made, the players switch roles with the former goalie now trying to score from the same spot. If successful, no letter is given. If unsuccessful, the player receives the letter "H." As with *Basketball Horse*, the game continues until one player has the word HORSE spelled against him.

# SOCCER BULL

**INTRODUCTION & PURPOSE:** *Soccer Bull* is somewhat similar to the game of Keep Away, except now the skills of kicking and trapping replace throwing. The simple rules and strategy makes this game appropriate for children of all ages.

**NUMBER OF PLAYERS:** 4 players (larger groups can play separate games simultaneously)

**SUGGESTED AGE LEVEL:** 7-17 years of age

**EQUIPMENT:** 1 soccer ball

**HOW TO PLAY:** Three players stand in a triangular-shaped formation about 10 to 15 feet apart from each other. One player is designated as the chaser (or the "Bull"), and stands in the middle of the triangle. On a starting signal, the players begin passing the ball from one player to another while the Bull is in pursuit of the ball. The Bull attempts to touch or intercept the ball with his feet or body. If successful, the Bull switches positions with the player who last touched the ball. A player also becomes the Bull if a passed ball goes past him and outside the playing area.

The objective is to last the game without becoming a Bull.

**VARIATION:** This game can be played with only three players by allowing the passers to move about in a designated playing area. The skill of dribbling is also utilized in this version.

# SOCCER CROQUET

**INTRODUCTION & PURPOSE:** This fun game is played much like regular croquet, except players are now kicking soccer balls between cones rather than using regular croquet equipment.

Besides being an activity that develops kicking accuracy, *Soccer Croquet* also reinforces game concepts and strategy used in the sport of croquet.

**NUMBER OF PLAYERS:** 2 to 4 players can play on one course; set up multiple courses for larger groups

**SUGGESTED AGE LEVEL:** 8-17 years of age

**EQUIPMENT:** 1 soccer ball for each player; 14 cones (or stakes)

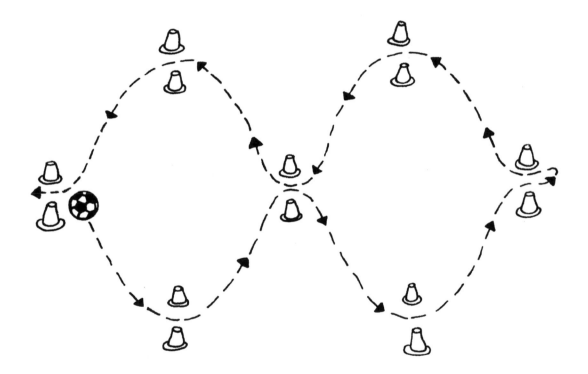

**HOW TO PLAY:** The rules and strategy of this game are much like regular croquet. The objective is to be the first player to the halfway point, turn around, and return home. Each player must kick his ball through the cones (in the direction shown above) before advancing to the next "wicket". As in regular croquet, everyone has the right to knock away another player's ball with his own. A player is allowed to kick again after hitting his ball through a wicket; otherwise, players alternate turns kicking.

**VARIATION:** Depending on the space available, the croquet course can be as large as you want it to be. Consider designing a course with a different configuration.

# ONE-ON-ONE SOCCER

**INTRODUCTION & PURPOSE:** The more "touches" a child has in practicing soccer skills, the sooner and greater the degree of skill development. Game leaders will find this partner activity accomplishes the goal of providing maximum individual dribbling and kicking practice opportunities.

*One-On-One Soccer* does not require a large playing area (making it ideal for backyards), and its simple rules/strategy makes it an appropriate learning activity for all age levels.

**NUMBER OF PLAYERS:** 2 players (larger groups can play games simultaneously on individually marked playing areas)

**SUGGESTED AGE LEVEL:** 6-17 years of age

**EQUIPMENT:** 1 soccer ball, 2 cones (or similar objects to represent goals)

**HOW TO PLAY:** The playing area consists of two cones placed approximately 30 feet to 50 feet apart. The distance can vary depending on the age of the players and available space. There are no boundary lines.

The two players start by facing each other (a couple of feet apart) in the middle of the playing area. One player is designated to kick off first. The objective is to dribble the ball toward the opponent's cone and kick it so it touches the cone. If successful, one point is scored and the ball is brought back to the middle for another kickoff. The player who did not score starts with the ball on the kickoff. Players can steal the ball anytime after the kickoff.

Touching the ball with the hands is a violation and results in the other player taking possession of the ball.

# TWO-ON-TWO SOCCER

**INTRODUCTION & PURPOSE:** Like *One-On-One Soccer*, this game offers numerous opportunities (or ball "touches") for children to practice their dribbling, kicking, trapping, defense, and passing skills.

Another advantage of this game is that far less space is required than regular soccer, and there is no need for marking boundary lines.

**NUMBER OF PLAYERS:** 4 players

**SUGGESTED AGE LEVEL:** 6-17 years of age

**EQUIPMENT:** 1 soccer ball, 4 cones (or similar objects to substitute for soccer goals)

**HOW TO PLAY:** Place two cones about 10 feet apart at each end of the playing area for goals. The goals should be around 60 feet apart (however, this distance can vary according to the age/skill level of the players). There are no boundary lines.

This game is played much like regular soccer with the exception being there are two players on a team, and no boundary lines. A kickoff in the middle starts the game. The objective is to score by kicking the ball between the cones (and below the top of the cones). After each score, the ball is placed in the middle of the field and the team that was scored upon kicks off. Since there are no goalies, both players on offense should be actively involved in advancing the ball down the field.

Players can move anywhere with the ball since there are no boundary lines. (However, a score can be made only by kicking the ball from the inside of the playing area.)

**VARIATION:** Have one player on each team play the goalie position. The other two players play one-on-one against each other. Rotate positions after each score.

# Section 4

# SOFTBALL GAMES

The sport of softball was invented by the YMCA in 1900 as a safer and more convenient alternative to baseball for children. Today the sport is enjoyed around the world by people of all ages.

The games in this chapter are adaptable to any outdoor setting (most of the games do not require a softball field) and concentrate on developing the three major skill areas of softball—throwing, catching, and batting. These fun activities are sure to have both children and adults saying "LET'S PLAY BALL!"

# GLOSSARY OF SOFTBALL TERMS & SKILLS

**BACKSTOP:** The protective fence located behind home plate.

**BASE:** The name given to the three bags and plate in the infield. There are first, second, third bases and a plate called home base.

**BASE ON BALLS:** When a batter receives four balls he is able to freely advance to first base.

**BASE PATH:** An imaginary line that runs three feet to either side of a direct line between the bases.

**BASES LOADED:** A term used when base runners occupy first, second, and third bases.

**BASE RUNNER:** An offensive player located on either first, second, or third base.

**BATTER'S BOX:** The area close to home plate in which the batter must stand.

**BATTING ORDER:** The order in which the members of a team will bat.

**BUNT:** A type of hit that is not swung at, but rather tapped so that the ball rolls slowly away from the batter's box.

**CATCHER:** The player behind home plate who receives the pitch from the pitcher.

**CENTER FIELDER:** The defensive player located in middle part of the outfield.

**COUNT:** A term used to indicate the number of balls and strikes on a batter.

**DEFENSE:** The team out in the field.

**DOUBLE:** A batted ball that results in the batter stopping safely at second base.

**DOUBLE PLAY:** When two base runners, or a base runner and the batter, are called out on the same play.

**DUGOUT:** The term used to describe the area where the team is located during the game. Offensive players who are not batting have to stay in the dugout until it is their turn to be on deck.

**ERROR:** A throwing or catching mistake made on the defensive team.

**FIELDER'S CHOICE:** When a defensive player chooses to put out a base runner rather than the batter.

**FIRST BASEMAN:** The defensive player located near first base.

**FLY BALL:** A ball that is hit up into the air and never touches the ground.

**FOUL BALL:** A hit made by the batter that does not stay in fair territory.

**FOUL TIP:** A batted ball that goes straight to the catcher and is caught.

**FORCE OUT:** A base runner is called out when a defensive play results in the fielded ball going to a base (before the base runner) that the base runner had to advance to in order to be safe. The fielders do not have to tag the runner, only the base.

**FULL COUNT:** A term used to indicate that the batter has three balls and two strikes.

**GRAND SLAM:** A home run hit with the bases loaded (a base runner is on all three bases).

**GROUNDER:** A batted ball that rolls along the ground.

**HOME RUN:** A batted ball that results in the batter circling all four bases for a run scored.

**INFIELD:** The fair territory located within the four bases.

**INNING:** The name given to a particular part of the game. The major leagues haves nine innings to a game.

**LEFT FIELDER:** The defensive player that is located beyond the infield on the left side.

**OFFENSE:** The team that is batting.

**ON DECK:** The term used to describe the next batter awaiting his chance to bat.

**OUT:** When the defensive team retires the batter or a base runner.

**OUTFIELD:** The fair territory located beyond the infield.

**OVERHAND THROW:** A ball thrown from above the shoulder area.

**PINCH HITTER:** A substitute batter.

**PITCHER:** The player who throws the ball to the batters.

**PLAY BALL:** A term used by the umpire signifying the start or resumption of play.

**POP UP:** A ball hit high but short into the infield area.

**RBI:** Stands for run batted in. Used to describe a batter who hits a ball that allows a base runner to score on a batted ball.

**RIGHT FIELDER:** The defensive player located in the right part of the outfield.

**SACRIFICE:** The term used to describe a play in which the batter is called out but the batted ball allows a base runner to advance to the next base.

**SECOND BASEMAN:** The defensive player located to left side of second base.

**SHORTSTOP:** The defensive player located in the infield between second and third bases.

**SINGLE:** A batted ball that results in the batter safely stopping at first base.

**SLIDE:** The term used to describe a base runner who attempts to touch a base with his legs, feet, or hands by going down on the ground (while running).

**STEALING:** A base runner trying to advance to the next base at the same time the pitcher is throwing to the batter.

**STRIKE ZONE:** The area above home plate between the batter's knees and armpits.

**TAG:** To touch a base runner with the ball, or to touch a base.

**TAG UP:** A base runner can attempt to advance to the next base on a long fly if he touches the bag (base) after a defensive player has caught it. If he tries to run to the next base before the fly ball is caught, he can be put out by a defensive player touching the base he was supposed to tag up.

**THIRD BASEMAN:** The defensive player located to the left side of third base.

**TRIPLE:** A batted ball that results in the batter stopping safely on third base.

**TRIPLE PLAY:** A batted ball that allows the defensive team to have three called outs.

**UNDERHAND THROW:** A ball thrown from a hand that is projected upward from the thigh area. The pitcher (in softball) is required to execute this type of throw when throwing to the batters.

**WALK:** A free advancement to first base when the batter has four balls.

# CATCH 22

**INTRODUCTION & PURPOSE:** *Catch 22* is a simple, but challenging game of "catch" designed to help the younger-age players develop throwing accuracy and catching skills. Depending on the specific throwing skill being emphasized, either the underhand or the overhand throw can be used.

**NUMBER OF PLAYERS:** 2 players (multiple pairs can play simultaneously)

**SUGGESTED AGE LEVEL:** 6-10 years of age

**EQUIPMENT:** 1 softball, 2 gloves

**HOW TO PLAY:** Begin with two players standing about 15 feet to 20 feet apart. This distance can vary depending on the age and skill level of the players. The players throw the ball (either overhand or underhand) to each other trying to be as accurate as possible. A thrown ball to the opponent's chest area (between the shoulders and waist) counts for 2 points. This is the area in which players should be aiming at. A thrown ball that forces the other player to jump, bend over, or move his feet to catch it counts for 1 point. A ball that is way off course and cannot be caught results in no points. The players add up their points during play. The objective is to be the first player to reach 22 points.

# PICKLE

**INTRODUCTION & PURPOSE:** In a regulation baseball/softball game, a base runner is in a "pickle" when caught between two bases with the possibility of being tagged by one of the two fielders guarding the bases. This unique situation creates a "game" within a game!

The skills of throwing, catching, and base running are all practiced in this simple but exciting activity.

**NUMBER OF PLAYERS:** 3 players (larger groups can play multiple games simultaneously)

**SUGGESTED AGE LEVEL:** 6-18 years of age

**EQUIPMENT:** One baseball/softball (or any similar size ball), 2 gloves (optional if using a soft, cushioned ball), 2 bases (or substitute any flat object to be used as a base marker)

**HOW TO PLAY:** Set two bases about 30 feet to 50 feet apart on a soft, dry area of grass. Two players (fielders) are to stand by the bases with a third player (the base runner) positioned halfway between the bases. One of the two fielders begins with a ball.

The two fielders start the game by throwing the ball back and forth, while at the same time, running toward the base runner so a tag can take place. The objective for the base runner is to reach one of the two bases safely without being tagged by one of the fielders. If the base runner is tagged before reaching a base safely, then the three players rotate positions. However, if the base runner successfully reaches a base, then play resumes again with the players in the same positions. The base runner only becomes a fielder again when tagged.

# SOFTBALL 21

**INTRODUCTION & PURPOSE:** The rules and strategy of *Softball* 21 add fun and competition to the practice of fielding fly and ground balls. A regular softball field is not required, but a large open area is needed for the longer hit balls.

**NUMBER OF PLAYERS:** 4 players

**SUGGESTED AGE LEVEL:** 8-14 years of age

**EQUIPMENT:** 1 softball, 1 bat

**HOW TO PLAY:** The players decide a batting order. Start with the player designated as the first batter positioned across from the other three players who are in fielding positions. The distance between the batter and fielders can vary depending on the age and skill level of the players. The batter begins by self tossing the ball up in the air and hitting it to any of the fielding players. The fielders attempt to catch the batted ball without error for points. A fielder is awarded 3 points for catching a fly ball, 2 points for catching a hit ball on one bounce, and 1 point for catching a grounder. After each batted ball, the players rotate positions with the next designated batter switching places with the previous batter. The objective is to be the first player to reach exactly 21 points.

**VARIATION:** Consider using a batting tee, especially if the players are having difficulty hitting a self-tossed pitched ball.

# HOME RUN DERBY

**INTRODUCTION & PURPOSE:** As the name of this game implies, the emphasis here is hitting the ball as far as possible. Besides batting, other skills developed through this activity include catching and pitching.

**NUMBER OF PLAYERS:** 4 players

**SUGGESTED AGE LEVEL:** 9-14 years of age

**EQUIPMENT:** 1 softball, 1 bat, 2 bases (or cone markers)

**HOW TO PLAY:** The game is played on a regular softball field or an open playing area with two cone markers about where first and third base would be located. A restraining line is drawn from first to third base. One team starts on offense as the pitcher and batter. The two defensive players stand in the field.

The pitcher throws underhand to his teammate (batter) who attempts to hit the ball beyond the restraining line. The batter is allowed up to three pitches to hit the ball. The batter is out if he fails to hit the ball, if a batted ball fails to reach the restraining line, or if a batted ball is fielded without error by one of the fielders. The batter receives 1 point if the unfielded batted ball lands beyond the restraining line but stays in the infield, and 2 points if the hit goes into the outfield. After an out or successful hit, the batter switches positions with his teammate (pitcher). The two offensive players continue in this fashion until they have 3 outs. As with regular softball, the teams switch roles after 3 outs. The objective for each team is to accumulate more points than the opponent.

# CRICKET BALL

**INTRODUCTION & PURPOSE:** This game contains elements of both softball and cricket (a very popular sport in Europe). The similarity of the skills used in both sports–throwing, catching, and batting–create a terrific cultural and skill-building learning experience for children.

**NUMBER OF PLAYERS:** 4 players (set up additional playing areas for larger groups)

**SUGGESTED AGE LEVEL:** 8-14 years of age

**EQUIPMENT:** 1 softball (or whiffle ball), 1 cone, 1 base, 1 bat

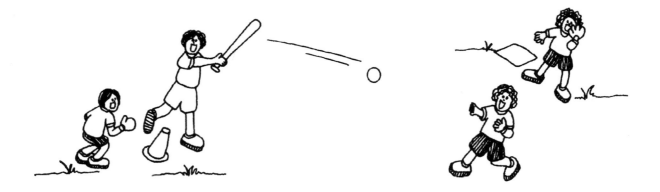

**HOW TO PLAY:** Set up a playing area with a cone and base placed in a straight line approximately 40 feet apart. This distance can vary depending on the age and skill level of the players. Assign the four players a starting position of batter, catcher, fielder, and pitcher.

The pitcher begins by throwing the ball toward the cone, which the batter is standing in front of and to the side. If the pitched ball hits the cone, a strike is called on the batter. A batter is ruled out if he has three strikes called on him. If the batter hits the ball, he attempts to run to the far base and back, without stopping, before the catcher is thrown the ball. If successful, the batter scores a run for himself. If unsuccessful, the batter is ruled out. Unlike regular softball, tagging the runner and catching fly balls do not count as outs.

Players rotate positions after each out or run. The batter moves to fielder, the fielder to pitcher, the pitcher to catcher, and the catcher becomes the new batter.

The objective is to end the game with the highest number of runs scored.

# ONE-ON-ONE SOFTBALL

**INTRODUCTION & PURPOSE:** *One-On-One Softball* is a great activity for introducing the younger-aged child to the sport of softball. The major skills of batting, fielding, and base running are all enhanced by this activity.

Because this game requires only two players, the parent/teacher will find it a perfect choice for the backyard or small space setting.

**NUMBER OF PLAYERS:** 2 players (set up additional playing areas for larger groups)

**SUGGESTED AGE LEVEL:** 6-10 years of age

**EQUIPMENT:** 1 batting tee, 1 softball (or whiffle ball), 1 bat, 1 cone (or a base substitute)

**HOW TO PLAY:** Mark off a playing area with a batting tee representing home base and a cone approximately 30 feet directly in front of the tee as a base. This distance can vary on the age and skill level of the participants. One player starts as the batter while the other player stands as a fielder.

The batter's objective is to hit the ball out into the field, run to the cone, and back to the tee (touching each one) before the fielder tags the tee. Meanwhile, the fielder attempts to retrieve the ball, run to the tee, and tag the tee with the ball before the batter has returned. A point is awarded to the batter if he beats the fielder to the tee. Likewise, the fielder is rewarded with the point if he is the first one back to the tee (with the ball in hand). The players reverse roles after each play and continue in this fashion. Unlike regular softball, this game rewards good defensive plays as much as good offensive plays. The objective is to have more points than the opponent at the end of play.

**VARIATION:** Consider changing the scoring system to that of regular softball. An out is given to the batter if he doesn't make it back to the tee first. After three outs, the players reverse roles. A point (or "run") is given only on the plays in which the batter successfully makes it back to the batting tee first.

Another variation is to have an adult or game leader pitch the ball instead of using the batting tee. The adult/game leader should not be involved as one of the two players (fielding the ball for example), but rather as a substitute for the tee only. The skill of batting from a tee to hitting a pitched ball is a natural leading up softball progression for children. This game is a great opportunity to introduce this skill.

# TRIPLE ACTION SOFTBALL

**INTRODUCTION & PURPOSE:** *Triple Action Softball* is essentially *One-On-One Softball* (page 84), but now three players are participating at once, with each player being a "team." Game leaders will find this activity to be a natural instructional progression from *One-On-One Softball*.

This game develops throwing, catching, batting (using a tee) skills, and introduces for the first time the concept of defensive players working together to get a batter out.

**NUMBER OF PLAYERS:** 3 players (set up additional areas for larger groups)

**SUGGESTED AGE LEVEL:** 6-10 years of age

**EQUIPMENT:** 1 softball (or a whiffle ball), 1 bat, 1 batting tee, 1 cone (or base)

**HOW TO PLAY:** Set up a playing area with a cone approximately 30 feet to 40 feet directly across from the batting tee. This distance can vary depending on the age and skill level of the players. Designate one player to start as the fielder, one player as the pitcher, and one player to bat first. The pitcher does not pitch, but does stand in front of the fielder closest to the batter.

The game begins with the batter hitting the ball off the tee into the field. The batter wants to run to the cone and back to the tee (touching each one) before the defensive players retrieve the ball and tag the tee. The batter scores a run for himself if he safely makes it to the tee. If not, no run is awarded. The two defensive players can work together to get the runner out by throwing the ball to each other, or one player can simply retrieve the ball and run to the tee.

The players rotate positions after each play. The batter moves to fielder, the fielder goes to pitcher, and the pitcher becomes the next batter. Play continues in this fashion throughout the game. The objective is to finish with more runs than the other players.

**VARIATIONS:** Consider changing the scoring system to that of regular softball. An out is given to the batter if he doesn't make it back to the tee first before the defensive players. He would continue to bat until he has three outs. After the third out, the players rotate positions in an order determined before the start of the game. A point, or run, is awarded only on the plays in which the batter successfully makes it back to the batting tee first.

Another version is to have an adult, or the game leader, pitch the ball instead of using the batting tee. This person's role is only to pitch (no fielding allowed) and act as a substitute for the use of the batting tee. The progression of batting from a tee to hitting a pitched ball is a natural leading up skill for children. This game variation would be an opportune time to introduce this skill.

# TWO-ON-TWO SOFTBALL

**INTRODUCTION & PURPOSE:** This game is a natural instructional progression from *One-On-One Softball* and *Triple Action Softball*. All of the major softball skills used in those games are utilized in this activity, but now the skill of base running is introduced.

Two-On-Two Softball does not require a regular softball field, making it ideal for any open space area. It can also be played inside a gymnasium with a whiffle ball and bat.

**NUMBER OF PLAYERS:** 4 players (set up additional playing areas for larger groups)

**SUGGESTED AGE LEVEL:** 8-17 years of age

**EQUIPMENT:** 2 bases, 1 bat, 1 softball (or a whiffle ball), 1 batting tee

**HOW TO PLAY:** Place two bases about 40 feet apart, with a batting tee set next to one of the bases. Designate one team (two players) to bat first with the other two players playing defense in the field.

The game begins with the batter hitting the ball out into the field. The batter's objective is to make it safely to the far base, where he can choose to stop and wait for the next batter to hit him home, or to the far base and back home without stopping. A run is awarded each time a player runs to the far base and back to home base. A batter is put out if a fielder catches a fly ball or if a runner is tagged. A batter can also be put out if the fielding team tags the far base before the runner arrives (this introduces the concept of the "force" out). There are no steals or strikeouts. After three outs, the teams switch positions.

**VARIATION:** Instead of using a batting tee, consider having the pitcher underhand toss the ball to the batter. The game leader can also pitch for both teams, thereby freeing up the two defensive players to play anywhere in the field.

88

# RACQUET
# & NET GAMES

This chapter of skill-building games is designed for the sports requiring a racquet and/or a net–volleyball, badminton, tennis, and pickleball. All of these activities can be played indoors or outdoors, and require only modest space.

Following the inclusive-style instructional model, these small group games are designed for maximum participation while developing skills in a fun and meaningful setting.

# GLOSSARY OF RACQUET & NET GAMES TERMS & SKILLS

## BADMINTON

**ALLEY:** An 18 inch wide area on each side of the court used for doubles play.

**AROUND THE HEAD:** An overhead forehand stroke taken when the shuttle is on the backhand side of the body.

**BACK ALLEY:** Area between the baseline and the doubles long service line.

**BACKCOURT:** Back one-third of the court.

**BACKHAND:** Stroke made on the nonracquet side of the body.

**BIRD (BIRDIE):** Alternate name for the shuttlecock.

**CARRY:** Shuttlecock (or birdie) illegally stays in contact with the racket during the stroke.

**CENTER LINE:** The midline dividing the service courts.

**CLEAR:** High shot that goes over an opponent's head and lands close to the baseline.

**CROSSCOURT:** A shot hit diagonally into the opposite court.

**DOUBLE HIT:** Racquet illegally contacts the shuttle twice in one swing.

**DRIVE:** A shot that is hit parallel to the ground and is too low for the opponent to smash.

**DROP:** A shot that barely clears the net.

**FAULT:** A violation of the rules resulting in either the loss of serve or points for the server.

**FORECOURT:** The area of the court between the net and short service line.

**FOREHAND:** Stroke made on the racquet side of the body.

**GAME POINT:** The final point allowing a server to win the game.

**INNING:** The part of a game during which a team or player retains the service.

**LET:** A time out or stoppage of play due to violations or interference.

**LOVE:** A term used to indicate a zero in scoring.

**MATCH:** A series of three games that determines the winner.

**MATCH POINT:** Point that, if won by the server, wins the match.

**MIDCOURT:** The middle third of the court.

**RECEIVER:** The player to whom the shuttlecock is served.

**SERVER:** The player who puts the shuttlecock into play.

**SHUTTLECOCK:** A feathered plastic or nylon object that is volleyed back and forth over the net.

**SIDE OUT:** When a serve is lost.

**SMASH:** A fast, downward overhead stroke.

**UNDERHAND STROKE:** Stroke that is hit upward from below shoulder level.

## TENNIS

**ACE:** A serve that is not touched by the opponent.

**BACKHAND:** A stroke in which the player turns so that the racket arm faces the net before bringing the racket forward and across the body to meet the ball.

**BASE LINE:** The line on either end of the court representing the outer limits of the length of the court.

**DEUCE:** A tie at 40. Since two points must win a game, play continues from deuce until one player leads by a margin of two points.

**DOUBLE FAULT:** When both serve attempts fail and the opponent wins the point.

**DROP SHOT:** A soft hit that drops barely over the net.

**FAULT:** Called if the ball is served into the net, or if it strikes the net before hitting the opponent's court outside the service box or before leaving the court completely.

**FOREHAND:** A shot in which the player pivots the body so that the shoulder of the nonracket arm faces the net. The player then swings the racket forward to meet the ball.

**LET:** Happens when the ball touches the net and falls into the diagonally opposite service box. The server is allowed to serve again.

**LOB:** A high, soft return hit behind an opponent who is close to the net.

**LOVE:** A term used to indicate zero points.

**SMASH:** A powerful shot often used to return a lob. The shot is hit in a similar manner as a serve.

**VOLLEY:** When a player strikes the ball before it bounces. The volley is most often used when a player is located close to the net.

# VOLLEYBALL

**ACE:** A serve that results in a point.

**ADD OUT:** The team that has scored a point following a tie at scores over 14 points.

**BLOCK:** A defensive play by one or more players used to stop a spiked ball.

**BUMP:** A pass made with the forearms.

**COURT:** A 30' by 30' playing area divided by a net and centerline.

**DEUCE:** Any tie score of 14 points or more.

**DIG:** A recovery pass from a spiked or powerfully hit ball.

**FOUL:** A violation of the rules.

**GAME POINT:** The last point in a game.

**NEWCOMB:** The term used in a game variation in which catching and throwing replaces setting and bumping.

**ROTATION:** A clockwise movement of players prior to the new serve

**SERVE:** A hit used by the player in the back-right position to put the ball into play.

**SET PASS:** A pass usually made over the head toward a hitter.

**SIDE OUT:** When the serving team fails to win the point or makes an illegal play.

**SPIKE:** A downward, powerful hit that resembles the overhand serve.

**TEAM:** Normal regulation rules call for six players–three in the front and three in the back row.

# BIRDIE IN THE AIR

**INTRODUCTION & PURPOSE:** *Birdie In The Air* requires little space and is played without a traditional court and net. The easy-to-understand game strategy makes it an appropriate activity for most age levels.

Badminton striking skills and cooperation are developed in this game.

**NUMBER OF PLAYERS:** 2-4 players (play several games simultaneously for larger-sized groups)

**SUGGESTED AGE LEVEL:** 9-17 years of age

**EQUIPMENT:** 1 birdie, 1 racket for each player

**HOW TO PLAY:** Have the players form a circle with each player about 2 feet to 3 feet apart. If only two players are playing, have the two face each other about 10 feet apart. One player starts with a birdie.

On a starting signal, the player with the birdie self-hits it underhanded into the air toward the other players. The players try to keep the birdie in play as long as possible without letting it land on the ground, and without making a double hit. Players are to keep track of their highest number of consecutive hits. For competitive play, the objective is to be the group (or individual) with the highest number of consecutive hits without a mistake.

# KEEP IT UP

**INTRODUCTION & PURPOSE:** This game is played very much like its badminton counterpart *Birdie In The Air* (page 93). Of course, in this game, volleyball passing skills replace badminton skills. *Keep It Up* requires little space and is played without a regulation court and net. The simplicity of the rules and strategy make it a perfect learning experience for the younger players.

Besides the development of passing skills, *Keep It Up* also enhances the social skills of cooperation and teamwork.

**NUMBER OF PLAYERS:** 2-4 players (play several games simultaneously for larger-sized groups)

**SUGGESTED AGE LEVEL:** 9-17 years of age

**EQUIPMENT:** 1 volleyball (or beach ball)

**HOW TO PLAY:** Have the players form a circle with each player about 4 feet to 5 feet apart. If only two players are playing, have the two face each other about 12 feet apart. One player starts with the volleyball.

To begin, the player with the volleyball tosses it up in the air and overhead passes to one of the players in the group. The players try to keep the volleyball in play as long as possible without letting it land on the ground, and without making an illegal pass (double hits, catching the ball, etc). Each contact with the ball counts as a point and the players are to keep track of their highest number of consecutive hits. Players have to start back at zero once the ball lands on the ground or an illegal pass has been made. For competitive play, the objective would be to have a higher number than other player or groups.

Encourage high passes so players can better position themselves to make contact.

# NO RULES TENNIS

**INTRODUCTION & PURPOSE:** *No Rules Tennis* is an ideal introductory experience for children. As the title suggests, just about anything goes–however, there are a few rules.

All of the major tennis skills are developed in this activity.

**NUMBER OF PLAYERS:** 2 players for singles play; 4 players for doubles

**SUGGESTED AGE LEVEL:** 8-12 years of age

**EQUIPMENT:** 1 ball, 1 tennis racket for each player

**HOW TO PLAY:** *No Rules Tennis* is played on a regular tennis court. For singles play, one player stands on each side of the net. For doubles play, two players stand on each side. One player is designated to serve first.

The game is played much like regulation tennis with the following exceptions:
1) A ball may bounce any number of times before it's played. As long as it keeps bouncing, the ball remains alive and in play. The play ends once the ball starts to roll.
2) A player can "bubble" a ball on his racket any number of times. That is, he can bounce it repeatedly off the strings of his racket before sending it over the net.
3) For doubles play, a player can hit the ball to a teammate any number of times before hitting it over the net.
4) For doubles play, the serve can be "helped" over the net by a teammate if it appears to be short of the net.
5) The server can serve anywhere on his court within 7 feet of the net.

Regular tennis scoring rules apply.

# NO NET BADMINTON

**INTRODUCTION & PURPOSE:** Your want to play badminton—but, you don't have a net? *No Net Badminton* is the answer for this dilemma. As the name implies, this is regulation badminton without a net. Because there is no net, children are going to experience a higher level of success.

With the exception of the slam shot, all of the major badminton skills are practiced in this activity.

**NUMBER OF PLAYERS:** 2-4 players, depending on whether you're playing singles or doubles

**SUGGESTED AGE LEVEL:** 9-17 years of age

**EQUIPMENT:** 1 birdie, 1 racquet for each player

**HOW TO PLAY:** A regulation badminton court of 45 feet by 25 feet is needed. The game can be played outdoors or indoors. There is no net, but a center line (representing the net) should be drawn the middle of the court. Place one player on each side, or two players on each side if playing doubles.

The rules for play are exactly like those of regular badminton (see page 102). The only exception is that no overhead hits are allowed. This rule is mainly to prevent the unfairness of a slam shot being taken because of the absence of a net. The birdie must always be hit with an upward projectory.

For a one-game match, play would continue until one player has scored 21 points (and wins by at least 2 points). Regular best of three game matches are played to 15 points.

# TWO-ON-ONE TENNIS

**INTRODUCTION & PURPOSE:** This game offers a unique solution for the tennis setting that has three players. The game is played with many of the same rules of regulation tennis, but with a "King of the Mountain" approach to scoring.

**NUMBER OF PLAYERS:** 3 players

**SUGGESTED AGE LEVEL:** 9-17 years of age

**EQUIPMENT:** 1 ball, 1 tennis racket for each player

**HOW TO PLAY:** *Two-On-One Tennis* is played on a regulation tennis court. Players decide a serving rotation. Two players start on the doubles court (the players chosen to serve second and third), while the other plays the singles court (the player designated to serve first).

For the most part, regular tennis rules apply throughout the game. However, only the player in the singles court serves and scores points. Once the server commits a fault, the players rotate positions with the player chosen to be the second server switching with the previous server. That player will continue to serve and score points until he commits a fault. At that time, the third player takes over the singles court and serves the ball. Play continues in this fashion throughout the game with each player attempting to stay in the singles court as long as possible.

The scoring is different than regulation tennis. A server receives 1 point for each successful play. The first player to score 9 points wins.

# VOLLEYBALL DOUBLES

**INTRODUCTION & PURPOSE:** Since there are only two players on each team, *Volleyball Doubles* offers a higher level of player movement and ball contact opportunities than regular volleyball. Additionally, the slow-moving beach ball makes it easier for players to react to the ball. *Volleyball Doubles* can be played just about anywhere–in the gymnasium, backyard, beach, park, etc.

All of the major volleyball skills are reinforced and developed in this exciting game.

**NUMBER OF PLAYERS:** 4 players (set up additional courts for larger groups)

**SUGGESTED AGE LEVEL:** 9-17 years of age

**EQUIPMENT:** 1 volleyball net, 1 beach ball

**HOW TO PLAY:** It is advisable for game leaders to delay the playing of this game until all the major volleyball skills have been introduced and practiced. *Volleyball Doubles* is essentially two-on-two volleyball with a few rule changes.

The server begins play by serving the ball over the net. The players on the other team attempt to hit the ball back over the net without letting it hit the ground, or causing it to go out of bounds. Because a beach ball is much bigger than a volleyball, a few rule changes are to be implemented:

1. A serve can be "helped" over the net by a fellow teammate.
2. Players can hit the ball to themselves two times before passing it to a teammate or over the net.
3. Teams can take up to five hits to get the ball over the net (either a serve or volley).

Other than the above changes, regular volleyball rules are to be followed. Only the serving team can score points. The objective is to be the first team to reach 15 points with at least a 2 point advantage.

# NEWCOMB DOUBLES

**INTRODUCTION & PURPOSE:** *Newcomb Doubles* is a throwing and catching version of *Volleyball Doubles* (see previous game). This game allows children to experience success early, which is important for developing a long-term motivation for playing volleyball. It also gives children a chance to learn the many volleyball rules and strategies before mastering the striking skills.

**NUMBER OF PLAYERS:** 4 players (2 on each team)

**SUGGESTED AGE LEVEL:** 8-12 years of age

**EQUIPMENT:** 1 volleyball net, 1 volleyball

**HOW TO PLAY:** Two players begin on each side of the volleyball net. *Newcomb Doubles* is played very much like regular volleyball except throwing and catching replace the standard striking passes. The objective is to throw the ball over the net so it strikes the ground on the opponent's side, and to catch and send back any ball thrown by the opposing team.

The game begins with a serve (a thrown ball) by one team. Players on the receiving team attempt to catch it before it hits the ground. A player must throw from the spot of the catch. No walking with the ball is allowed and a player has only three seconds to throw. Each team can catch and pass among themselves a maximum of three times. Play continues until one team commits an error by failing to make a catch, making more than three passes before sending the ball over the net, or by throwing a ball into the net or out of bounds.

Regular volleyball scoring is used. The objective is to be the first team to reach 15 points with at least a 2-point advantage.

# FOUR SQUARE VOLLEYMINTON

**INTRODUCTION & PURPOSE:** *Four Square Volleyminton* is essentially a four-team volleyball game, with each player being a team. The smaller court size (approximately the size of a badminton court) makes it possible for individual players to retrieve any type of hit.

All the volleyball skills (striking, serving, bumping, etc.) are practiced in this activity.

**NUMBER OF PLAYERS:** 4 players

**SUGGESTED AGE LEVEL:** 9-17 years of age

**EQUIPMENT:** 1 volleyball (or beach ball), 2 badminton nets (or ropes)

**HOW TO PLAY:** Set up a playing area designed like a four square with the two badminton nets (see diagram above). One player stands in each of the four courts.

A designated player starts by serving behind the back line into any of the other three courts. Players use bumps and overhead hits to keep the ball from landing inside their court area. Basic volleyball rules apply with one exception—a player can hit a ball twice in succession to himself before it goes over the net.

The player serving the ball continues to serve until he commits a violation, or until another player strikes the ball into a court and it is not returned properly. Violations can result in a loss of serve if the server committed the violation, or a point for the server if his serve or passes are not returned properly.

Violations include:

1. The server failing to serve the ball over the net.
2. Serving the ball out of bounds.
3. A player striking the ball more than two times in a row before passing it over the net.
4. A player passing the ball out of bounds.
5. Any player touching the net during play.
6. Any player crossing underneath the nets during play.
7. A player illegally striking a ball (for example, catching and throwing)

The objective is to be the first player to reach 15 points.

**VARIATIONS:**  Consider mixing the rules of Four Square into the above game. Designate each of the four courts as  "A," "B," "C," and "D." The player in Court A serves the ball to one of the three players. Play continues with players using bumps and overhead passes to keep the ball from landing inside their court area. If a player hits the ball out of the four square boundary, or if the ball lands in his square, that player goes to Court D, and all of the other players move up one square. See the diagram below.

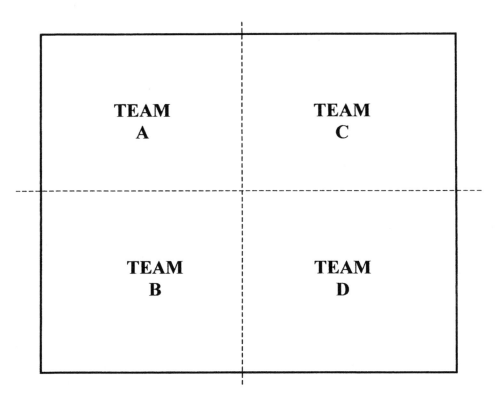

Another variation is to play the above game with badminton racquets and balloons instead of volleyball striking. The same rules as explained above would apply. The only difference is that now each player has a racquet and badminton striking skills are used. Using a balloon slows down the action so that players have sufficient time to react to the hits.

# BADMINTON

**INTRODUCTION & PURPOSE:**   Although *Badminton* has become a highly skilled, competitive sport at the international level, it remains a casual backyard favorite for many families. The game is played with either two players (one-on-one) or four players (doubles). The low number of required participants makes it an ideal homeschool physical education experience.

**NUMBER OF PLAYERS:**  2 players (singles) or four players (doubles)

**SUGGESTED AGE LEVEL:**  9-17 years of age

**EQUIPMENT:**  1 birdie, 1 net, 1 racquet for each player

**HOW TO PLAY:**  Mark off a badminton court that measures about 45 feet by 25 feet for doubles play and slightly smaller for singles play. A service line should also be marked about 3 feet to 4 feet behind the net on both sides of the court.

For singles play, the server stands behind the service line and hits the birdie underhand with the racquet to the opposite side of the opponent's court. If he returns the birdie over the net, a volley ensues until the birdie falls to the ground or goes out of bounds. When this happens, if the server is at fault, the serve goes to the opponent. If the receiver makes the error, a point is scored for the server, who serves again and continues to do so until he makes an error. Points can only be scored by the serving player.

Players cannot touch the birdie more than once in succession. If the birdie hits the net, it is still in play as long as it goes over and remains within the boundary lines.

For a one-game match, play would continue until one player scores 21 points (and wins by at least 2 points). Regular best of three game matches are played to 15 points.

Doubles play progresses the same as above, except when the first player on a team loses the serve, it goes to his partner before going to the other team.

Other basic rules of badminton play include:

1. Any birdie hitting the boundary lines is considered in bounds.
2. In singles, the birdie must land in the long, narrow court. In doubles, it must land in the short, wide court.
3. In doubles, once the serve has been returned, the full court is used.
4. The server is permitted only one attempt to put the birdie into play.
5. In singles, the serve is made from the right side of the court when the server's score is an even number.
6. In doubles, the first serve is always started from the right court whenever a team acquires the serve from its opponent.
7. The server must call the score after each score.
8. A match is the best of three games.
9. Players change sides of the court after each game.
10. The winner of the previous game serves first for the next game.

# PICKLEBALL

**INTRODUCTION & PURPOSE:** *Pickleball* is a popular and fast-growing game in many school physical education curriculums. It is also gaining popularity as a lifetime sport with many families. The striking and movement skills children gain from this activity are very similar to those developed in tennis and badminton.

   *Pickleball* is easy to learn and provides children a fun alternative to other racquet sports.

**NUMBER OF PLAYERS:** 2 players for singles play, 4 players for doubles

**SUGGESTED AGE LEVEL:** 9-17 years of age

**EQUIPMENT:** 1 badminton or tennis net, 1 pickleball or whiffle ball, 1 paddle for each player

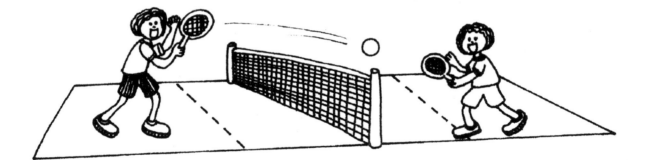

**HOW TO PLAY:** The official court size is 20 feet by 44 feet for both singles and doubles. This is the same size as a badminton court, but with a three-foot high net. A seven-foot "non-volley zone" extends across the court on both sides of the net.

   The server stands behind the service line and underhand hits the ball, in the air, diagonally crosscourt past the non-volley zone. Normally only one serve attempt is allowed. However, a second serve can be attempted if the ball touches the net on the serve and lands in the proper service court. At the start of each new game, the first serving team is allowed only one fault before giving up the ball. Thereafter, both members of each team will serve and fault before the ball is turned over to the opponents. When the receiving team wins the serve, the player in the right hand court will always start play.

   The receiver cannot volley the serve. In other words, the ball must bounce before being returned. Likewise, the server must let his opponent's return bounce once on his side after a serve. After the two bounces have occurred, the ball can be either volleyed or played off the bounce. Players rally back and forth until a fault is made. The winner of the volley has the option of serving first or receiving first. A minimum of three hits must be made for the rally to be valid.

A game is played to 11 points and a team must win by at least 2 points. Only the serving team scores points. A player who is serving will continue to do so until a fault is made by his team.

Faults that result in a loss of serve or point include:
1. Volleying the ball before the double bounces have occurred.
2. Stepping into the non-volleying zone and volleying the ball. However, a player can return a ball that lands in the non-volley zone if he lets it bounce first.
3. Serving or hitting a ball into the net.
4. Serving or hitting the ball out of bounds.

For doubles play, special rules apply to serves and faults. A point is scored by the serving team each time the fault is made by the receiving team. When the serving team wins a point, its players switch courts and the same player continues serving. When the serving team makes its first fault, players will stay in the same court and the second partner will then serve. When they make a second fault, they will stay in the same court and turn the ball over to the other team. Players switch courts only after scoring.

**VARIATIONS:**  The following are some suggestions for modifying the game for young children.
1. On the serve, allow the ball to bounce before striking.
2. Eliminate volleys and require all balls to bounce before hitting.
3. Eliminate the crosscourt serve rule when playing doubles. Just have the children concentrate on getting the ball over the net and past the non-volley line.
4. Along with eliminating volleys (and requiring balls to bounce), consider getting rid of the non-volley zone. The bounce rule would make this zone obsolete.
5. Consider playing without paddles. Players would be allowed to catch and throw the ball.

# RECREATIONAL SPORT GAMES

This chapter introduces a wealth of activities to help children learn a variety of lifetime sports and games. The parent/teacher will discover that participation in these activities will help children refine their movement skills, enhance their fitness levels, and provide significant social growth. The long term goal of using these learning activities is to launch a lifetime of recreational enjoyment for children.

107

# GLOSSARY OF TERMS AND SKILLS USED IN RECREATIONAL SPORT GAMES

## BOCCE

**BOCCE END LINE:**  The mark that a player must not step past before releasing the ball.

**BOULE:**  The name given to the throwing ball when playing Petanqua Bocce.

**INSIDE:**  The name given to the team that has their ball land closest to the jack. Whenever a team gets "inside" it must bowl second behind the "outside" team.

**JACK:**  The name applied to the target ball.

**OUTSIDE:**  The name given to the team that has their ball the longest distance from the jack. This team bowls next ahead of the "Inside" team.

**PALLINO:**  The name given to the throwing ball when playing the official regulation game. In a game version called Petanqua Bocce, the throwing ball is called a boule.

**PUNTATA SHOT:**  A bocce ball that is gently rolled as close as possible to the target ball from a crouched position.

**RAFFA SHOT:**  A strong shot executed close to the ground. Its purpose is to dislodge an opponent's ball or to disrupt a formation.

**VOLO SHOT:**  A bocce ball that is tossed in the air with a reverse spin. The reverse spin causes the ball to stop at the point of impact.

## BOWLING

**ALLEY:**  The name given to the surface of the bowling playing area.

**BOWLING FOUL LINE:**  The mark that determines the beginning of the lane. Players can not cross this line when bowling.

**FRAME:**  The box in which scores are entered.

**GUTTER BALL:**  A ball that goes into a depression on the outsides of the lane.

**HANDICAP:**  Pins given to individuals or teams in an attempt to equalize competition.

**OPEN:**  A frame that doesn't have a strike or spare.

**PERFECT GAME:** Twelve strikes in a row with a count of 30 pins per frame resulting in a score of 300.

**SPARE:** Occurs when all the pins are down after the second ball.

**STRIKE:** Occurs when all ten pins are knocked down on the first ball.

# CROQUET

**CROQUET:** To strike one's own ball when in contact with a roqueted ball. The player places one foot on his own ball and hits the ball to send the opponent's ball in any direction.

**MALLET:** The name applied to the bottom of the striking club.

**RICOCHET:** Occurs when two or more balls are displaced with one hit of the mallet.

**ROQUET:** Occurs when a player strikes his own ball so that it contacts an opponent's ball.

**ROVER:** The name applied to a player who has hit his ball through all the arches (but not the final post), but continues to play. This player can hit his ball anywhere to assist his team and drive back the opposition.

**WICKET:** The name of the arch the ball must travel through.

# GOLF

**ACE:** A hole in one.

**BIRDIE:** One under par for the hole.

**BOGEY:** One over par for the hole.

**DOUBLE BOGEY:** Two shots over par for the hole.

**DOUBLE EAGLE:** Three shots over par for the hole.

**EAGLE:** To score two under par for the hole.

**FAIRWAY:** The playing area between the tee and the green, which does not include hazards.

**FORE:** A warning to the other players that a ball may hit them.

**GREEN:** The area of short grass surrounding the hole.

**HANDICAP:** The number of strokes a player is given to adjust his score to that of a standard scratch.

**HOLE IN ONE:** Occurs when the ball goes straight into the hole from the tee shot.

**PAR:** The number of shots a low handicapper should take for a hole or round. Par for a hole is calculated by the number of shots needed to reach the green plus two for the putting. Par for a round is measured by adding all of the hole's pars together.

**PENALTY STROKE:** A stroke added to a player's score due to a rule infringement.

**PUTT:** A close shot taken on the green toward the hole.

# HORSESHOES

**FOUL LINE:** The line players must not cross when throwing.

**INNING:** A portion of the game when two players pitch two shoes each.

**LEANERS:** When a shoe lands against the stake but does not fall down flat. Leaners are worth 1 point.

**PIT:** The area in which the stake is placed. The size of the pit should be 31 to 36 inches wide and 43 to 72 inches deep.

**PITCH:** The name applied to the throw of the shoe.

**RINGER:** When the shoe lands fully encircled on the stake. Ringers are worth 3 points. However, a player is awarded 4 points if he has the closest shoe and a ringer together.

# EAN AG HORSESHOES

**INTRODUCTION & PURPOSE:** The traditional game of Horseshoes can be intimidating for many children. The heavy horseshoes and the distance needed to throw them makes it very difficult for children to experience success. In this modified game, beanbags (softer and lighter in weight than horseshoes) and hula hoops (a bigger target than the traditional stake) take the place of the regular equipment. These changes create a Horseshoe-type game that even the youngest of players can enjoy.

**NUMBER OF PLAYERS:** 2-4 players to a game

**SUGGESTED AGE LEVEL:** 6-9 years of age

**EQUIPMENT:** 2 hula hoops, 4 beanbags

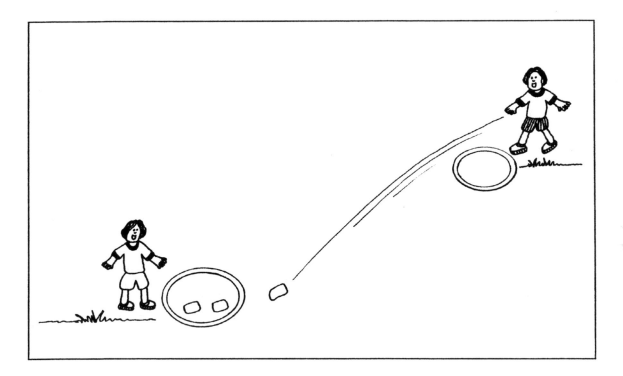

**HOW TO PLAY:** Place two hula hoops approximately 15 feet to 30 feet apart. The distance can vary depending on the age and skill level of the players. Each player starts with two beanbags. Players decide a throwing order.

This activity is played much like the traditional game of Horseshoes, except beanbags and hula hoops replace the shoes and stakes. When throwing, players must stay behind the hoops. Each player is allowed two throws at a time. The objective is to throw the beanbag so it lands inside a hula hoop for a "ringer."

If keeping score, a ringer counts as 3 points. A beanbag that ends up being the closest to a hoop (without being a ringer) counts as 1 point. The first player (or team) to score 15 points wins the game.

# INDOOR BEANBAG BOWLING

**INTRODUCTION & PURPOSE:** This is a terrific instructional choice for introducing young players to the game of bowling. The advantages of this activity include the familiarity children have with the underhand toss, and beanbags being much easier to handle than a bowling ball. Additionally, the bowling pins can be moved as close as needed toward the throwers to assure success.

**NUMBER OF PLAYERS:** 2-4 players to a bowling lane

**SUGGESTED AGE LEVEL:** 6-10 years of age

**EQUIPMENT:** 2 beanbags for each player, 3 bowling pins

**HOW TO PLAY:** Set up a bowling lane with the three pins about 20 feet from a throwing line. The pins should be in a tight rectangular shaped formation. One player stands behind the pins ready to set up the pins after being hit, while the other players stand in a file behind the throwing line.

The first bowler takes a couple of steps and underhand throws the beanbags toward the bowling pins. The objective is to gain a strike by knocking over all three pins, or to knock over as many as possible by the second throw. After the second throw, the bowler takes the place of the pin set-up player with the pin set-up player going to the throwing line. Each bowler is allowed up to two throws per frame, with 10 frames in each game. The game objective is to knock over the highest number of pins by the end of play.

# AERO IC BOWLING

**INTRODUCTION & PURPOSE**: This game develops the rolling skill used in bowling, and has the added attraction of providing plenty of continuous movement for the participants.

**NUMBER OF PLAYERS**: 2 players (larger groups can play multiple games simultaneously)

**SUGGESTED AGE LEVEL**: 6-17 years of age

**EQUIPMENT**: 1 bowling pin (or substitute an empty 1 liter soft drink container) and 1 ball (a bowling ball or a playground type ball)

**HOW TO PLAY**: Place a bowling pin about 30 feet away from a spot where the roller is to stand. One player starts as the roller while the other stands behind the pin. The roller begins the game by rolling the ball toward the pin. The goal is to gain a "strike" by knocking down the pin. After releasing the ball, the roller runs toward the pin and switches places with the player standing behind the pin (who sets up the pin if knocked down). The players switch positions after each roll.

If keeping score, the first player to reach a predetermined number of strikes wins the contest.

# FRISBEE BOWLING

**INTRODUCTION & PURPOSE:** Frisbee throwing (using bowling strategies and score-keeping) is the principle skill enhanced in *Frisbee Bowling*. This game can be played in any outdoor or large indoor setting.

**NUMBER OF PLAYERS:** 2-4 players to a contest (or a single player can play by himself by attempting to improve his score with each game)

**SUGGESTED AGE LEVEL:** 6-17 years of age

**EQUIPMENT:** Any number of plastic bowling pins (or substitute plastic liter soft drink containers); 1 frisbee; score sheets (available at many bowling alleys)

**HOW TO PLAY:** Set up a "bowling lane" with the bowling pins (any number from 1-10) about 30 feet to 40 feet from the spot where the frisbee thrower stands. The objective is to hit the pins and knock as many of them down with each throw. The game is played exactly like regulation bowling with the exception that a frisbee replaces the bowling ball.

Each bowler is allowed two throws per frame, for ten frames, in each game. Players take turns between bowling and setting up the pins for the next thrower.

Scoring is the same as in regulation bowling.

# SOCCER BOWLING

**INTRODUCTION & PURPOSE:** *Soccer Bowling* is bowling using soccer kicking skills. Besides developing kicking accuracy, young players learn the strategy and terminology of bowling.

**NUMBER OF PLAYERS:** 2-4 players (set up additional bowling lanes for larger groups)

**SUGGESTED AGE LEVEL:** 6-14 years of age

**EQUIPMENT:** 10 bowling pins, 1 soccer ball

**HOW TO PLAY:** Set up a bowling lane with the 10 bowling pins approximately 30 feet from the spot where the kicker stands. This distance can vary depending on the age and skill level of the players. One player stands behind the pins ready to set up the knocked over pins while the other players stand in a file behind the kicking line.

*Soccer Bowling* is essentially the game of bowling with the ball being kicked instead of rolled. The first kicker attempts to kick and knock down as many pins as possible. The objective is to gain a "strike" by knocking all the pins down, or to knock over as many as possible by the second kick. After the second kick, the kicker takes the place of the pin set-up player with the pin set-up player going to the kicking line. Each bowler is allowed two kicks per frame, with 10 frames in each game. Scoring is the same as in bowling. If available, players can use score sheets to help keep track of the score.

# FRISBEE GOLF

**INTRODUCTION & PURPOSE:** *Frisbee Golf* is one of the author's favorite activities to teach, as well as play! Besides being a physical education game, it's also a terrific family leisure-time activity. The skills developed in *Frisbee Golf* include frisbee throwing and golf scorekeeping.

**NUMBER OF PLAYERS:** 1-4 players to a course

**SUGGESTED AGE LEVEL:** 9-14 years of age

**EQUIPMENT:** 1 frisbee for each player, 9 hula hoops (or ropes), 9 cones

**HOW TO PLAY:** Set up a "golf course" by placing the hula hoops (or jump ropes) approximately 30 feet apart in a scattered formation. This distance can vary depending on the age and skill level of the players. Place a numbered cone inside each hula hoop to indicate the hole number. Players decide a throwing order.

The first player throws a Frisbee toward hole #1, trying to land it inside the hula hoop. In order, the other players do the same. Players continue in this fashion until all have "holed out." The player with the lowest score (that is, the fewest throws attempted to place the frisbee inside the hula hoop) is allowed to throw first for the next hole. The objective is to finish the course in the fewest number of "strokes" (or throws).

**VARIATION:** Instead of using hula hoops for the holes, consider using natural or man-made objects such as tree trunks, poles, etc. Almost anything located in a backyard, playground, or park setting can be used with a little imagination. In fact, the children will enjoy designing their own "putt-putt" course.

116

# SOCCER GOLF

**INTRODUCTION & PURPOSE:**  This combination-sport game develops the skill of soccer kicking using golf strategies and scorekeeping. Besides being an excellent physical education activity, this fun-packed game could also serve as a recess and family leisure time activity.

*Soccer Golf* is best played outdoors–however, it does not require a regulation soccer field or golf course.

**NUMBER OF PLAYERS:**  Any number from 2-4 players

**SUGGESTED AGE LEVEL:**  8-16 years of age

**EQUIPMENT:**  1 soccer ball per player, 9 hula hoops (or ropes), 9 cone markers

**HOW TO PLAY:**  Design a playing area that resembles a golf course by placing the hula hoops approximately 30 feet to 40 feet apart in a scattered formation. This distance can vary depending on the age of the players and the amount of playing space available. Place a numbered cone (1-9) inside each hula hoop to indicate the hole number. Players decide a kicking order.

The first player kicks a soccer ball toward hole #1, trying to land it inside the hula hoop. In order, the other players do the same. Players continue in this fashion until all have "holed out." The player with the lowest score (that is, the fewest kicks attempted to place the ball inside the hula hoop) is allowed to kick first for the next hole. The objective is to finish the course in the fewest number of "strokes" (or kicks).

# CROQUET GOLF

**INTRODUCTION & PURPOSE:** *Croquet Golf* is essentially a miniature golf game played with croquet equipment. In addition to being an appropriate physical education game, many children will find it a favorite recess or leisure time activity.

*Croquet Golf* enhances croquet striking and golf scorekeeping.

**NUMBER OF PLAYERS:** 2-4 players to a course

**SUGGESTED AGE LEVEL:** 8-17 years of age

**EQUIPMENT:** 9 wickets (numbered 1-9 with tape), 1 mallet and ball for each player

**HOW TO PLAY:** Design a playing area that is similar to a mini-golf course by placing the wickets (numbered 1-9 with tape) approximately 15 feet to 20 feet apart in a scattered formation. Players decide a playing order.

The first player tees off by hitting the croquet ball toward the first hole (wicket #1). In order, the other players do the same. Players continue in this fashion until all have "holed out." The player with the lowest score (that is, the fewest strikes attempted to hit the ball through the wicket) is allowed to tee off first for the next hole. The objective is to finish the course with the fewest number of "strokes."

# THROW GOLF

**INTRODUCTION & PURPOSE:** In addition to developing the skill of throwing, *Throw Golf* is a great introduction to golf strategy and scorekeeping. A variety of balls or objects can be used in performing the underhand and overhand throws. (For indoor play, beanbags would be an ideal choice.)

Although the game description below uses hula hoops and cones for golf holes, *Throw Golf* can also be played with a "putt-putt" theme using a variety of outdoor objects such as tree trunks, poles, etc.

**NUMBER OF PLAYERS:** 2-4 players to a course

**SUGGESTED AGE LEVEL:** 7-14 years of age

**EQUIPMENT:** 1 ball for each player (a softball, whiffle ball, beanbag, etc.), 9 hula hoops (or jump ropes can be substituted), 9 cones

**HOW TO PLAY:** Design a playing area that resembles a golf course by placing the hula hoops approximately 30 feet to 40 feet apart in a scattered formation. This distance can vary depending on the age of the players and the amount of playing space available. Place a numbered cone (1-9) inside each hula hoop to indicate the hole number. Players decide a throwing order.

The first player throws a ball (or beanbag) toward hole #1, trying to land it inside the hula hoop. In order, the other players do the same. Players continue in this fashion until all have "holed out." The player with the lowest score (that is, the fewest throws attempted to place the ball inside the hula hoop) is allowed to throw first for the next hole. The objective is to finish the course with the fewest number of "strokes" (or throws).

119

# CROQUET

**INTRODUCTION & PURPOSE:**   The game of *Croquet* has long been a recreational favorite with children and adults. As a physical education game, croquet develops hand-eye coordination, while the game strategy and rules serve as a leading-up experience to other striking sports such as golf.

**NUMBER OF PLAYERS:**  2-4 players to a course

**SUGGESTED AGE LEVEL:**  8-17 years of age

**EQUIPMENT:**  1 complete croquet set

**HOW TO PLAY:**  Set up a playing area with the wickets and posts in a formation as shown in the diagram above. Players pick a color and always hit in the order of blue, red, yellow, green, and orange.

The first player begins by placing the ball on the ground at a spot that is about one-third the distance between the starting post and the first wicket. The ball must be struck, and not pushed, with the face of the mallet. If a player drives the ball through the first two wickets, he is awarded two extra strokes. Extra strokes are allowed for driving the ball through a wicket, hitting another ball, or hitting a stake. Once a player's turn is over, the next player in line begins. Play continues in this fashion with each player attempting to drive the ball through the wickets to the halfway post and back. The objective is to be the first player to complete the course.

Below are special rules that apply to the game of *Croquet*. Depending on the age of the players, some of these rules can be introduced at a later time.

1.  A player forfeits a turn if he plays out of turn or hits the wrong ball.
2.  A player can either croquet or continue to play if his ball displaces another ball and passes through a wicket. (See the glossary for a full description of croquet.)
3.  Only one extra stroke is allowed if both a ricocheting and croqueting ball pass through a wicket. (See the glossary for a description of ricochet.)
4.  Regardless of how many balls are hit on a single stroke, only one additional stroke is given. The player must croquet all hit balls or none.
5.  A player can croquet the same ball twice, but only after the croquet has passed through a wicket or hit a stake.
6.  A player roqueting a ball does not have to croquet it.
7.  In the event a ball is hit outside the playing area, it is replaced one mallet length inside the outer boundary where it originally went out.

# OUTSIDE BILLIARDS

**INTRODUCTION & PURPOSE:** With a little imagination, it is possible to play the game of billiards in an outdoor setting without a billiards table! *Outside Billiards* combines the skill of kicking, as used in soccer, with the cognitive strategy of billiards.

**NUMBER OF PLAYERS:** 2-4 players to a playing area

**SUGGESTED AGE LEVEL:** 8-17 years of age

**EQUIPMENT:** 10 soccer balls, 1 playground ball, 12 cones

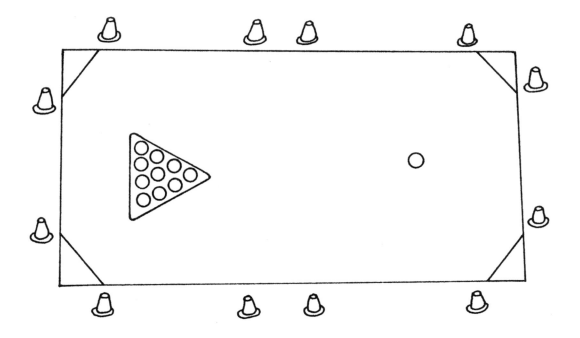

**HOW TO PLAY:** With the cones, mark off a playing area that is approximately 20 feet by 30 feet in size. Two cones are set two feet apart in the spots designated as the "pockets." The 10 soccer balls are set in a tight, triangular shaped formation at one end of the playing area, with the cue ball (playground ball) at the other end.

    The strategy used in this game is much like regular billiards. The goal is to pocket more shots than the opponent. The first player begins by kicking the cue ball toward the soccer balls, trying to knock one of them into a pocket (through the cones). Any player that successfully makes a shot is allowed to keep kicking until he misses. After a missed shot, the next player begins his turn.

    Occasionally, a soccer ball might travel outside the boundary lines during the course of the game. When this happens, take the ball and place it at the spot on the "table" where it went out of bounds.

    If playing two players to a team, each player alternates kicking chances. Scoring would remain the same as described above.

# CROQUET BILLIARDS

**INTRODUCTION & PURPOSE:** This combination-sport game develops the striking skill used in croquet with the cognitive strategy of billiards.

Despite its name, *Croquet Billiards* does not require a billiards table. Instead, this game uses an outdoor playing area shaped like a billiards table.

**NUMBER OF PLAYERS:** 2 players (set up additional playing areas for other couples)

**SUGGESTED AGE LEVEL:** 8-14 years of age

**EQUIPMENT:** 3 croquet balls, 1 croquet mallet, cones to mark off boundary lines

**HOW TO PLAY:** With the cones, mark off a playing area approximately 10 feet by 25 feet in size (shaped like a billiards table). Place two croquet balls toward the end of the playing area about a foot apart. The cue ball (also a croquet ball) is set at the opposite end. Players determine a striking order.

The first player strikes the cue ball attempting to hit one of the two balls. If successful, he is allowed a follow-up shot at the second ball. If he is successful at hitting the second ball, he is awarded a "billiard" (which counts as 1 point). The objective is to hit both balls in succession as often as possible. The first player to reach 15 billiards (or 15 points) wins the contest. After a missed shot, the next player begins his turn as in regular billiards.

The striking skill used in this game is the same technique used in croquet.

# BEANBAG BOCCE

**INTRODUCTION & PURPOSE:** *Beanbag Bocce* is a modified version of Bocce that uses beanbags instead of the traditional bocce balls. The beanbags allow children to experience the game of Bocce with equipment that is inexpensive, easy to use, and safe.

For indoor play, a hard surface works best as it allows the beanbag to slide. As a result, players will be able to practice the same rolling and throwing skills as those used in regular Bocce.

**NUMBER OF PLAYERS:** 2-4 players to a game (set up additional courts for larger groups)

**SUGGESTED AGE LEVEL:** 8-14 years of age

**EQUIPMENT:** 2 beanbags per player, 1 object to represent the center ball or marker (a hockey puck or a similar disk-like object works best)

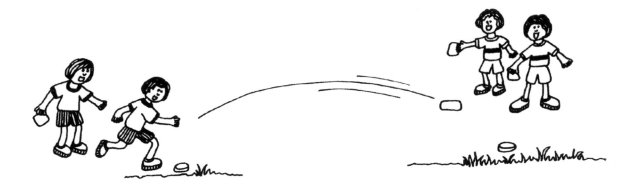

**HOW TO PLAY:** Mark off a playing area that is approximately 6 feet by 20 feet in size. One of the far ends is designated as the throwing line. Place a center marker toward the other end. Players determine a throwing order with each player holding two matching beanbags.

In turn, the players throw or slide their two beanbags at the center marker. The objective is to hit or have a beanbag land closest to the center marker. Scores are calculated after all the beanbags have been thrown. The player whose beanbag lands on the marker or closest to it receives 3 points. The next closest receives 2 points, and the third closest 1 point. Because each player has two throwing attempts, it's possible for a single player to receive two scores. Play continues in this fashion until one player has reached 15 points.

It is legal, and considered good strategy, to knock another player's beanbag away from the center marker during the course of the throws.

# MODIFIED BOCCE

**INTRODUCTION & PURPOSE:** This is a modified version of the popular Italian game of Bocce. Bocce is considered to be the front-runner to the modern game of bowling and is often used in this country by physical educators as a lead-up to that sport.

The rolling skills used in *Modified Bocce* are identical to those used in regular bocce, and much like bowling.

**NUMBER OF PLAYERS:** 2 players to a game (set up additional playing areas for larger groups)

**SUGGESTED AGE LEVEL:** 7-12 years of age

**EQUIPMENT:** 2 balls for each player, 1 center ball (the center ball should be a different type than the one the players are using)

**HOW TO PLAY:** Mark off a playing area that is approximately 6 feet by 20 feet in size. Designate one of the far ends as the throwing line. Place a center ball toward the other end. Each player starts with two balls, which should be a different type than the center ball. Examples of ball types include baseballs, softballs, croquet balls, etc. Players determine a throwing order.

In turn, the players throw or roll their two balls at the center ball. The objective is to hit or have a ball land closest to the center ball. If only one player hits the center ball, he is declared the winner of that round and is awarded 1 point. In the event more than one player hit the center ball, the players continue throwing/rolling until a winner is declared. If no center ball is hit, the winner is the player with his ball landing closest to it. A player who throws the ball in the air and hits the center ball would win over a hit made on a bounce or roll. Players continue in this fashion for 15 rounds (or any predetermined number of rounds).

# BOCCE CROQUET

**INTRODUCTION & PURPOSE:** This game develops the skill of bocce rolling using croquet equipment. Besides being a terrific physical education activity, *Bocce Croquet* is also an appropriate family leisure time backyard activity.

**NUMBER OF PLAYERS:** 2-4 players to a play area (set up additional playing lanes for larger-sized groups)

**SUGGESTED AGE LEVEL:** 7-14 years of age

**EQUIPMENT:** 1 croquet stake, 3 croquet wickets, 2 balls per player (croquet balls are ideal)

**HOW TO PLAY:** Set up a row of three wickets (about 6-12 inches apart) with a stake at the end. A rolling line should be designated approximately 20 feet away from the wickets. This distance can vary depending on the age of the players. Before starting, the players decide upon a rolling order. Each player begins with two balls.

In turn, each player attempts to roll his ball accurately enough so it makes it through all three wickets hitting the stake. A stake hit counts as 5 points. A ball that goes through all three wickets but does not contact the stake is worth 3 points. A ball going through two wickets earns 2 points, and a ball getting through one wicket earns 1 point. The objective is to be the first player to accumulate 15 points. A player should remove each of his previously rolled balls so the next roller has a clear field to the stake.

Players must roll their ball without touching the rolling foul line. A violation results in a loss of turn.

# Section 7

# PLAYGROUND GAMES

The games in this chapter give parents and game leaders a wonderful opportunity to make the recess break a meaningful and educational experience for children. In fact, recent studies have shown a direct correlation between exercise and academic performance.

A playground game/activity unit should be implemented yearly in the K-6 grade homeschool physical education curriculum to ensure that children have the tools to participate in healthy leisure-time activities.

# ONE-ON-ONE KICKBALL

**INTRODUCTION & PURPOSE:** One problem of regular kickball (played with a large group) is the sedentary nature of the game. Players spend much more time standing (either waiting a turn to kick, or for a ball to be kicked toward them) than they do moving. *One-On-One Kickball* eliminates this problem since there are only two players. Each participant is either running or kicking during the entire game.

**NUMBER OF PLAYERS:** 2 players (mark off additional playing areas for other pairs)

**SUGGESTED AGE LEVEL:** 6-12 years of age

**EQUIPMENT:** 1 playground ball, 2 bases (or cone markers)

**HOW TO PLAY:** Set two bases or cone markers approximately 20 feet to 60 feet apart (the distance can vary depending on the age/skill level of the players). One player starts as the kicker and stands near the base designated as home base. The other player is the pitcher.

The pitcher begins the game by gently rolling the ball toward the kicker. The kicker kicks the ball in any direction (there are no boundary lines), and begins running around the two bases. As he is running, the kicker counts the number of times he circles around the far base and back. The pitcher retrieves the ball and must touch one of the two bases (either by throwing or tagging) to stop the kicker from running. When finished, the kicker tells the other player how many times he circled the bases. The players then switch positions and play continues. The objective is to have the highest score.

**VARIATION:** Instead of using two bases or cones, consider using an actual softball field and/or a playing area with four bases. The kicker would need to run around four bases to score, and the pitcher has a choice of four bases to tag with the ball.

# TRIPLE ACTION KICKBALL

**INTRODUCTION & PURPOSE:** This game is essentially *One-On-One Kickball* (see previous game) with an additional fielder. This extra player introduces the concept of defensive players working together to put a kicker out.

**NUMBER OF PLAYERS:** 3 players (mark off additional playing areas for larger groups)

**SUGGESTED AGE LEVEL:** 6-12 years of age

**EQUIPMENT:** 1 playground ball, 2 bases (or cone markers)

**HOW TO PLAY:** Set the two bases or cone markers approximately 20 feet to 60 feet apart (the distance can vary depending on the age/skill level of the players). The three players decide a kicking rotation before starting. The player designated to kick first stands near the base or cone designated as home plate. The other two players are the pitcher and fielder.

The pitcher begins the game by gently rolling the ball toward the kicker. The kicker kicks the ball in any direction (there are no boundary lines) and begins running around the two bases. As he is running, the kicker counts the number of times he circles the far base and home plate. The pitcher and fielder retrieve the kicked ball and attempt to touch (either by throwing or tagging) one of the two bases to stop the kicker from running. When finished, the kicker tells the other two players how many times he circled the bases. The three players then switch positions (according to the predetermined rotation) and the game continues.

**VARIATION:** Instead of using two bases or cones, consider using an actual softball field and/or a playing area with four bases. The kicker would then need to run around four bases to score a point, and the fielders have a choice of up to four bases to tag with the ball.

# KICKBALL DOUBLES

**INTRODUCTION & PURPOSE:** *Kickball Doubles* is a natural learning progression of *One-On-One Kickball* and *Triple Action Kickball*. Similar to those games, *Kickball Doubles* does not require a regular softball field, making it ideal for any open space area.

The skills of kicking, rolling, base running, and catching skills are developed in this activity.

**NUMBER OF PLAYERS:** 4 players (2 on each team)

**SUGGESTED AGE LEVEL:** 6-10 years of age

**EQUIPMENT:** 2 bases, 1 playground ball

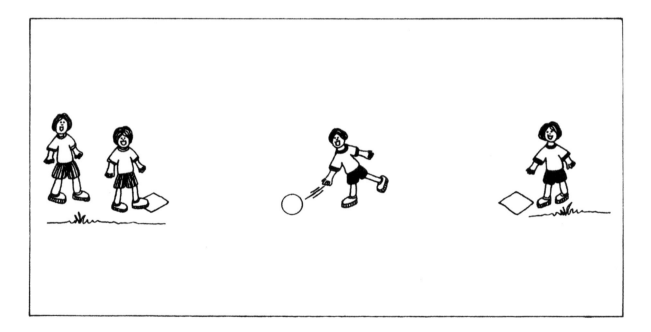

**HOW TO PLAY:** Place two bases about 40 feet apart. Designate one team (two players) to kick with the other two players on defense playing pitcher and fielder.

The pitcher begins the game by gently rolling the ball toward the kicker. The kicker kicks the ball in any direction (there are no boundary lines) and begins running. The kicker's objective is to make it safely to the far base, where he can choose to stop and wait for the next kicker to hit him home, or to the far base and back home without stopping. A run is awarded each time a player runs to the far base and back to home base. A kicker is out if a fielder catches a fly ball or if he is tagged while running the bases. A kicker is also out if the fielding team tags the far base before the runner arrives (a "force" out). The base runners can not steal bases, nor is there any "leading-off." After 3 outs, the teams switch positions.

**VARIATION:** Consider having the game leader pitch for both teams, thereby freeing up the two defensive players to play anywhere in the field.

# HOPSCOTCH

**INTRODUCTION & PURPOSE:** This is a classic playground game that has been played by children around the world for centuries. Although there are many different Hopscotch varieties, the objective is basically the same–to complete the course successfully without committing a foul.

**NUMBER OF PLAYERS:** 2 or more players

**SUGGESTED AGE LEVEL:** 6-12 years of age

**EQUIPMENT:** Chalk for marking a hopscotch course (if necessary), and a marker for each player (a stone, bottle cap, coin, etc.)

**HOW TO PLAY:** For American Hopscotch, use chalk to mark a basic course as shown in the diagram above.

The first player stands outside the court and tosses a marker into the space labeled #1. The marker must land completely within the space. If it touches any lines, the player forfeits a turn and goes to the back of the line.

When the marker lands correctly, the player jumps over the space containing the marker and lands on one foot in space #2. The player proceeds down the court by hopping on one foot where a single space exists, and straddling the court when two spaces are side by side. When traveling to the last space and back, he stops at the second space, picks up his marker from the first space and hops out. If this player has successfully completed his first turn without any fouls, he proceeds on his next turn to throw the marker into space #2 and so forth. Players should take turns, always starting where they left off. The objective is to be the first player to complete the course.

A player forfeits a turn if any of the following fouls are committed: 1) Failure to throw the marker fully inside the intended space. 2) Stepping on a line. 3) Hopping into a space that contains the marker. 4) Using the hands for support while picking up a marker.

# HANDBALL

**INTRODUCTION & PURPOSE:** *Handball* is another favorite activity of children that can be played with a partner (one-on-one) or as doubles (two-on-two). Like *Wall Ball*, the game is played against a wall adjacent to a paved or hard surface. In fact, many public playgrounds feature walls built specifically for this game.

Hand-eye coordination and striking skills are enhanced by this activity.

**NUMBER OF PLAYERS:** 2 players (or 4 players if playing doubles)

**SUGGESTED AGE LEVEL:** 9-17 years of age

**EQUIPMENT:** 1 handball or tennis ball, chalk to mark a court

**HOW TO PLAY:** Although a regulation handball court is 20 feet by 34 feet in size, many available play areas will not have these markings. Chalk can be used to draw lines, as well as a serving line that is normally 16 feet from the wall. These dimensions can be adjusted to the age and skill level of the players.

Both players stand in the middle of the court facing the wall, with one player designated to serve first. The server initiates the game by bouncing the ball once against the ground and hitting it, when it comes up, at the wall. The ball must bounce back over the serving line to be considered good. The server has two tries to make a good serve.

The other player tries to hit the served ball back against the wall. The ball can be hit after one bounce or while still on the fly. The ball is hit back and forth continuously between players until one fails to hit it, or hits it over the wall or out of bounds. If the non-serving player makes an error, the server scores a point. If the server makes the error, the serve goes to the other player. Only the server can score points. The objective is to be the first player to reach 21 points.

Sometimes one player will get in the way of the other when moving toward the ball. This is a foul and results in the serve being repeated if the non-serving player committed the foul, or the serve going to the other player if the server made the error.

**VARIATION:** If four players are available, consider playing two on two. Doubles play is basically the same as above, except only the partner closest to the ball may return it. Also, only the serving partner may be in the court while serving, but his partner can run back in as soon as the serve is made.

# TETHERBALL

**INTRODUCTION & PURPOSE:** *Tetherball* is a mainstay of the school playground and a popular backyard family activity. It's also perfect for the homeschooling family as it requires only two or four participants. Children develop hand-eye coordination and agility through the required striking skills.

**NUMBER OF PLAYERS:** 2 players (or 4 players if playing doubles)

**SUGGESTED AGE LEVEL:** 8-17 years of age

**EQUIPMENT:** 1 tetherball and a pole

**HOW TO PLAY:** A typical tetherball court is five feet in diameter, with a pole in the middle (see diagram above). Players must stay on there half of the court at all times.

The server begins by batting the ball with his hand either to the right or left. The opposing player attempts to bat the ball back in the opposite direction. Each player continues batting the ball back and forth, trying to wrap the ball completely around the pole in his direction. One point is awarded to the player who is successful at doing this. Play continues with the other player serving next. The objective is to be the first player to reach 10 points.

Players can only use their hands when batting the ball, and cannot touch the cord or pole during play. A violation results in a free serve for the opponent.

For doubles play, one player from each team assumes an alternate court position and must remain there during play. As the ball moves around the pole, each team attempts to wind the ball completely around the pole in the team's direction of play. Scoring is the same as in singles play.

For children just learning the game, consider allowing the ball to be caught before striking.

# WALL BALL

**INTRODUCTION & PURPOSE:** This is a classic playground game that children have long enjoyed playing. Besides improving throwing and catching skills, *Wall Ball* also develops agility and coordination.

**NUMBER OF PLAYERS:** 2 players (multiple games can be played simultaneously for larger groups)

**SUGGESTED AGE LEVEL:** 8-14 years of age

**EQUIPMENT:** 1 tennis ball, a wall, chalk

**HOW TO PLAY:** This game requires a wall and hard playing surface. With the chalk, mark a short line about five feet from the wall. Both players begin the game by standing anywhere behind the line. One player starts with the ball and is the first server.

The server begins by throwing the ball against the wall, letting it bounce once on the ground first. The opponent tries to catch the ball before it bounces more than once. If the opponent is successful, he becomes the next server. If a successful catch is not made, the server receives a point and continues serving.

All throws must clear the 5-foot short line, and must hit the ground before hitting the wall. If not, a fault is called and the other player is awarded the serve. Play continues in this manner with each player striving to achieve more points than the opponent.

Depending on the age and skill level of the players, consider moving the short line back to 10 feet to 15 feet.

# TRIANGULAR KEEP AWAY

**INTRODUCTION & PURPOSE:** Keep Away games have always been a popular playground activity for children. This variation, played with four participants, provides more ball contact opportunities than the larger-sized game variations.

*Triangular Keep Away* develops passing and catching skills. It also provides lots of healthy movement for the player in the middle.

**NUMBER OF PLAYERS:** 4 players

**SUGGESTED AGE LEVEL:** 7-13 years of age

**EQUIPMENT:** 1 playground ball, chalk (if necessary for marking lines)

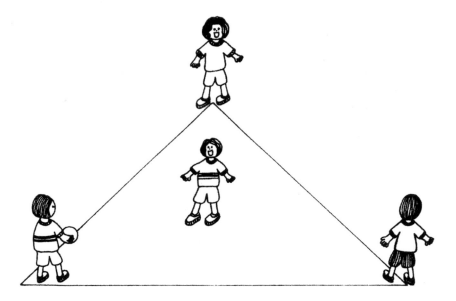

**HOW TO PLAY:** Mark a triangle approximately 10 feet to 12 feet long on the sides. Assign a player to each of the three corners and one player to stand in the middle. One of the corner players starts with the ball.

The player with the ball begins the game by passing the ball to one of the other corner players. The corner players attempt to pass the ball around, or through the triangle, without losing control of the ball. The passes can be of any type (chest, bounce, baseball, etc). Meanwhile, the middle player is attempting to steal, touch, or knock away a pass. If the middle player is successful (or if a corner player loses control of the ball), the last corner player to have touched the ball switches places with the middle player and the game continues. The objective is to avoid being a middle player.

Special rules need to be enforced for fair play. These include: 1) A corner player becomes a middle player if he is tagged while holding the ball, or if he has possession of the ball for more than five seconds. 2) An errand pass results in the passer, not the intended receiver, becoming the next middle player. 3) Corner players must stay in the corners and cannot run around the inside of the triangle. However, the middle player is free to move anywhere.

# TWO SQUARE

**INTRODUCTION & PURPOSE:** *Two Square* is sometimes referred to as "outside ping pong" because of the similarity of the rules and strategy. It's also the perfect alternative to *Four Square* (page 138) when only two players are available.

Striking skills and hand-eye coordination are enhanced by this activity.

**NUMBER OF PLAYERS:** 2 players

**SUGGESTED AGE LEVEL:** 6-12 years of age

**EQUIPMENT:** 1 playground ball, chalk (if necessary to draw lines)

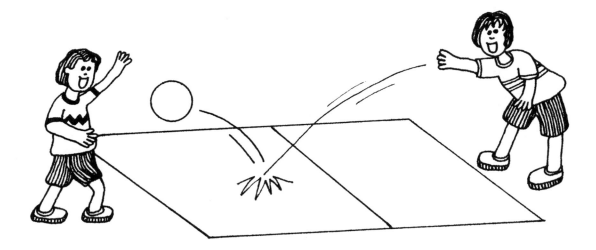

**HOW TO PLAY:** The playing area includes two adjoining squares as shown in the diagram above. Chalk can be used to draw lines if an existing court is not available. Start with a player standing in each square. The player in square #1 begins with the ball.

The overall objective of this game is stay in square #1. The ball is put into play when the player in square #1 bounces the ball once and hits it with an open hand (underhanded) into the other player's square. The serve is made from the serving line. The server must land the ball in the opponent's court unless the opponent chooses to hit it back before it bounces in his square. A serve landing on the inner line is a fault, while a ball landing on an outer boundary is considered good.

Players bat the ball back and forth until one player fails to return the ball, or commits a fault (that is, hitting the ball out of bounds, catching a ball, stepping into the opponent's square, or allowing the ball to touch any part of the body except the hands). If the server is at fault, he leaves and the other player takes square #1. The next awaiting player in line steps into square #2. The ousted player goes to the end of the waiting line.

If exactly two players are playing, consider adding ping-pong scoring rules. Only the server scores points, and he continues serving as long as he does not commit a fault. The objective is to be the first player to reach 21 points.

# FOUR SQUARE

**INTRODUCTION & PURPOSE:** *Four Square* is an expanded version of *Two Square* with more players and a larger court. This game develops striking skills and improves hand-eye coordination.

**NUMBER OF PLAYERS:** 4 or more players

**SUGGESTED AGE LEVEL:** 7-13 years of age

**EQUIPMENT:** 1 playground ball, chalk (if necessary)

**HOW TO PLAY:** The court consists of four equal squares labeled A, B, C, and D. The server's square (A) has a service line marked diagonally across the square. Before play, each of the players is to assume a standing position in one of the four squares. The player in square A is the server and starts with the ball. The player in this square always serves and must stay behind the line when serving.

The ball is served by dropping and striking it underhanded, with both hands, from the bounce into any of the other squares. If the serve hits a line, the server is out. The player receiving the serve must let it bounce once before hitting it into another square. Play continues until one player fails to return the ball or commits a fault.

A fault is any of the following:
1. Hitting the ball sidearm or overhand.
2. Landing a ball on a boundary line.
3. Stepping into another square to play the ball.
4. Catching or carrying a ball.
5. Allowing the ball to touch any body part except the hands.

When a fault has occurred, the players shift positions. If the server (A) commits a fault, he moves to square D, D moves to C, C moves to B, and the player in B becomes the next server. If playing with more than four players (players waiting in line outside the court), the player committing the fault leaves the court and goes to the back of the line. The player in front of the waiting line moves into square D, and the other three players move up one square.

The overall objective is to move up a square after each fault and eventually become the server.

**VARIATIONS:** The following are Four Square variations.

# CATCH FOUR SQUARE

In some cases, a player learning to play Four Square for the first time will enjoy more success by substituting catching and tossing in place of the normal serve and tap. Four Square rules apply, except each player catches the ball after the first bounce in his square and then tosses it underhanded into another square.

# BEANBAG FOUR SQUARE

This variation is played like regular Four Square, except plastic scoops and a beanbag replace the playground ball. Because this game requires catching a thrown beanbag with a scoop, the one bounce rule does not pertain to this game. Faults include (1) throwing the beanbag out of bounds, (2) landing the beanbag on a line, (3) touching or throwing the beanbag with anything other than the scoop, (4) having the beanbag fall out of the scoop, (5) and throwing with an overhand motion.

# PADDLE FOUR SQUARE

This variation is played like regular Four Square, except paddles (pickleball size) and a tennis ball replace the playground ball. Instead of striking the ball with the hands, players use paddles to hit the ball inside the squares. Faults include (1) allowing a ball to land inside one's square, (2) hitting the ball out of bounds, (3) landing a ball on a line, (4) and touching the ball with anything other than the paddle.

# AROUND THE WORLD FOUR SQUARE

This fun variation is played like regular Four Square with one exception–the ball has to be hit in a certain direction. For example, if the server hits the ball to the right, the ball must continue going around the square in that direction. The server can change the direction anytime the ball lands in his square by calling out "Left," or "Right." Continue play in this fashion until someone commits a fault. The faults are identical to those used in regular Four Square.

# BATTLE FOUR SQUARE

Regulation Four Square rules apply unless the server calls out "Battle!" before a serve. When this happens, the server can hit the ball to anyone, but the other players must always play the ball back to the server. This continues until a player commits a fault or the server calls out "Battle Over!" When this happens, play resumes as regulation Four Square.

# DOUBLES FOUR SQUARE

This variation calls for a total of eight players. Two players pair up and go to a square with one player standing inside the square and the other waiting outside the square.

Regulation rules pertain with one exception–partners switch in and out of their square throughout the game. As soon as one partner inside the square hits the ball, he quickly moves out allowing his partner (who has been waiting outside the square) to step in. Since regular Four Square rules are used, if one partner commits a fault, both partners would move to square D and the other teams would move up.

# KING SQUARE

This variation is much like Doubles Four Square described above, except both partners are now stationed inside the square. If possible, mark off squares that are slightly larger than those used in regulation Four Square. The rules and faults are the same used in regulation Four Square. Partners take turns hitting the ball without exiting the square.

# FOUR SQUARE TEAM TAG

**INTRODUCTION & PURPOSE:** This is one of those games that will keep children active for a long time! *Four Square Team Tag* combines the excitement of playing tag with the skills of throwing and catching.

**NUMBER OF PLAYERS:** 4 or more players

**SUGGESTED AGE LEVEL:** 7-13 years of age

**EQUIPMENT:** 1 foam ball, chalk for marking a four square court

**HOW TO PLAY:** Mark off a four square court as shown above. Divide the participants into two teams of 2-4 players each. Designate one team to start with the ball as the taggers. Players can stand anywhere inside the court.

The objective of the tagging team is to tag all the members of the opposing team. The game begins with the tagging team throwing the ball among themselves so that a member of the opposing team can be touched with the ball. The taggers can't move when they have the ball or throw the ball at an opponent. However, they can move without the ball in order to set up a quick catch and touch of an unsuspecting opponent.

Once tagged, a player must leave the court. However, this player can re-enter the game if a member of the tagging team drops a pass or makes a pass out of bounds. A dropped or incomplete pass also results in the other team taking possession of the ball and becoming the taggers. The game ends when one team has successfully tagged and forced out the members of the opposing team.

# FOUR SQUARE TAG

**INTRODUCTION & PURPOSE:** This is an adaptation of *Line Tag* (page 156), a game that uses the lines of a basketball court. *Four Square Tag* uses the same strategy, but now the lines of a four square court are used. This modification, along with *Two Square Tag* described below, creates a fun and exciting playground activity for small groups.

**NUMBER OF PLAYERS:** 3-4 players

**SUGGESTED AGE LEVEL:** 7-13 years of age

**EQUIPMENT:** 1 foam ball for tagging, chalk for marking a four square court

**HOW TO PLAY:** Mark off a four square court as shown above. One player begins as the "It" and stands on one of the court lines with a soft foam ball. The other players stand on a line anywhere around the court (this includes the middle lines as well).

On a starting signal, the "It" chases and attempts to tag one of the other players. All players, including the "It," have to stay on a line while fleeing and chasing. A tagged player takes the ball from the "It" and becomes the new tagger. The "Its" are not allowed to throw the ball. Play continues in this fashion until time is called. The objective is to avoid becoming an "It" as much as possible.

## TWO SQUARE TAG

*Two Square Tag* uses the lines of a two square court (see the court as shown on page 138). The strategies and rules are identical to those used in *Four Square Tag*.

# MORE P.E. GAMES
## *WITH A*
## *HOMESCHOOL TWIST!*

This chapter covers a variety of new games, as well as old favorites that have been modified to make them more appropriate for the homeschool physical education setting. These modifications still include the element of fun, but now valuable social skills, as well as movement and physical fitness skills are enhanced because of the inclusive-style changes.

# GAMES FOR ENHANCING MOVEMENT SKILLS

**INTRODUCTION & PURPOSE:** These games offer children an opportunity to use a variety of movement skills (skipping, galloping, sliding, jumping, hopping, running, etc.). The author has modified most of these traditionally large-group games to better meet the educational objectives of developing motor skills and movement.

**NUMBER OF PLAYERS:** 3 or more players

**SUGGESTED AGE LEVEL:** 6-10 years of age

**EQUIPMENT:** None

**HOW TO PLAY:** Before playing, children need to be adequately instructed on how to perform various motor skills, such as skipping, galloping, jumping, hopping, sliding, leaping, and running. Game leaders should also delay the playing of these games until the children have acquired the spatial awareness skills needed to travel safely in a group setting.

All of the games described below require a playing area that has two lines approximately 40 feet apart. The "It" (or a similar name depending on the game) stands in the middle with the rest of the players standing on a line. Follow the specific directions and rules for each game.

## LITTLE BROWN BEAR

Select one player to stand in the middle as the Little Brown Bear. The other players stand on a line facing the Little Brown Bear. The game begins with the Little Brown Bear calling out, "Who's afraid of the Little Brown Bear?" The other players respond with, "Not me!" The

144

Little Brown Bear then says "Well, then I want all of you to skip to the other side." The players must skip to the other safety line while the Little Brown Bear attempts to tag them. Tagged players become helpers and join the Little Brown Bear in the middle for the next turn. The Little Brown Bear should call out a different way to travel each time (galloping, running, etc.) The Little Brown Bear and his helpers must travel the same way as the fleeing players. The game ends when all the players have been caught.

# MARTIANS

Choose one player to be the Martian ("It") and have him stand in the middle of the playing area facing the lined players (the "Earthlings"). The game begins with the Earthlings chanting, "Martian, Martian, will you take us to the stars?" The Martian replies, "Only if you are wearing blue (or any color the Martian chooses to call out)." The Earthlings wearing the designated color may walk safely to the other safety line. At the same time, the players without that color must run (or any chosen method of traveling) and avoid being tagged by the chasing Martian. Any players who are caught must join the Martian and help catch the other players. The game ends when all the Earthlings have been caught.

# OCTOPUS

Choose one player to be the Octopus ("It") and have him stand in the middle of the playing area facing the lined players. The game begins with the Octopus calling out "Swim." The line players then run to the other safety line and try to avoid getting tagged by the chasing Octopus. Tagged players become tentacles ("helpers") of the Octopus and stand at the spot where they were tagged. A tentacle can't run, but they can tag others who come close enough with their outstretched arms. Players tagged by a tentacle also become tentacles. The game continues in this fashion until all the players have been caught. Vary the traveling movements throughout the game.

# SUNDAY

Select one player to be the "It" and have him stand in the middle of the playing area facing the lined players. The "It" begins the game by calling out any day of the week. However, on "Sunday," the line players must run to the other safety line avoiding the "It" who is attempting to tag them. A tagged player joins the "It" in the middle and becomes a helper for the next turn. Also, a player standing on the line who moves prematurely on any day of the week (except "Sunday") must also join the "It" in the middle. The game ends when all the line players have been caught. Vary the traveling movements throughout the game.

# TREES

Choose one player to be the "It" and have him stand in the middle of the playing area facing the lined players. Each time the It calls out "Trees," the line players must run to the other safety line while the It attempts to tag them. A tagged player becomes a helper (a "tree") and stands exactly at the spot where he was tagged (not in the middle). A "tree" cannot chase other players, but they can tag others who run close by with their outstretched arms. Players tagged by Trees also become Trees. The game continues in this fashion until all the players have become Trees. Vary the traveling movements throughout the game.

# STEP AWAY

**INTRODUCTION & PURPOSE:**  Are your players bored of playing ordinary "catch" in order to practice their throwing and catching skills? *Step Away* is a fun and challenging alternative to throwing and catching drills. Both the underhand and overhand throw can be used in this activity.

**NUMBER OF PLAYERS:**  2 players  (additional players can play simultaneously in pairs)

**SUGGESTED AGE LEVEL:**  6-13 years of age

**EQUIPMENT:**  1 piece of equipment for throwing (frisbee, whiffle ball, beanbag, football, foam ball, etc.), 2 cones (or similar objects to use as markers)

**HOW TO PLAY:**  Have two players stand about 6-8 feet apart with a cone (or similar marker) directly to the front and side of each one. One player is designated as the "thrower" and starts with a ball or throwing object. The playing area needs to be large enough for both players to be able to move backwards to a maximum throwing distance range.

 The objective is for the partners to successfully throw and catch the object, without dropping it, in order to move apart as far as possible. Each time a player successfully makes a catch, he moves his cone back one step. However, each time the throwing object is dropped or caught in front of the cone, the cone is moved toward the thrower one step. Only the catcher (not the thrower) moves their cone forward or backward during the game. Players continue throwing and catching to see how far apart they can eventually get.

 For competitive play against other teams, the objective is to be the pair with the longest throwing distance at the end of a designated time limit.

# DUCK DUCK GOOSE
## (One-On-One)

**INTRODUCTION & PURPOSE:** This partner activity is a modified version of the popular game *Duck, Duck, Goose*, which is traditionally played with a large group. The many advantages of this adaptation include a higher level of personal participation (less standing or sitting), less space is required, and only two players are needed. This is a wonderful game to use in the physical education lesson as part of a warm-up routine or as a closing activity.

**NUMBER OF PLAYERS:** 2 players (additional players can play in pairs)

**SUGGESTED AGE LEVEL:** 6-13 years of age

**EQUIPMENT:** None

**HOW TO PLAY:** Have two players stand facing each other in the middle of the safety lines. The safety lines are marked approximately 30 feet behind each player.

   The game begins with the two players exchanging a handshake. This is done after each turn to prevent players from starting too early (for example, one player calling out "Goose" from the very beginning before the other player is ready to run). After the handshake, the players can begin taking turns tapping each other on the shoulder saying either "Duck" or "Goose." Neither player moves when "Duck" is said. However, when a player says "Goose," he turns and runs toward his safety line with the other player in pursuit. The runner wins if he makes it to the safety line without being tagged first. However, the chaser is credited with the win if he tags the runner before the safety line. After each turn, the players return to the middle and play again.

   Players can keep score if they like. However, most children will find it's not necessary. As with other tag games, they'll probably want to just play for the fun of chasing and fleeing from each other.

# ROLL & RUN

**INTRODUCTION & PURPOSE:**  This chasing and fleeing game, played with dice, reinforces various mathematical skills. Don't be surprised if this fun activity leaves your children craving more "math time"!

**NUMBER OF PLAYERS:** 2 players (play multiple games simultaneously for larger groups)

**SUGGESTED AGE LEVEL:**  8-14 years of age

**EQUIPMENT:**  Foam blocks with numbers on each side. These can be purchased in many of the physical education catalogs that are available online and in print. You can also make these foam dices by using foam blocks and fabric bought at a fabric store. Another alternative is to use regular dice.

**HOW TO PLAY:**  Have two players stand facing each other about 3-4 feet apart. A safety line is marked about 30 feet behind each player. Designate one player as the "Odd" player, and the other as "Even." The game leader stands by the players with the two dice in hand.

Before rolling the dice, the game leader announces the mathematical function the players are to perform. For example, "Add the two numbers together that appear on the dice when they come to a stop." The game leader then rolls the dice between the players. If the answer is an even number, the "Even" player chases the "Odd" player back to his safety line. If the answer comes up odd, then the "Odd" player chases the "Even" player. A point is awarded to the chaser who successfully tags the runner before reaching the safety line. However, the point is awarded to the runner if he makes it to the safety line without getting tagged. After each turn, the players return to the middle and play again.

Other mathematical commands can include having the players subtract the smaller dice from the larger dice, and multiplying the two numbers displayed.

# STEAL THE BEANBAG
## (One-On-One)

**INTRODUCTION & PURPOSE:** This partner activity is a modified version of the popular game *Steal The Bacon*. The many advantages of this game (as opposed to *Steal The Bacon*) include a higher level of movement, less space is required, and only two players are needed. Children will love the chasing and fleeing aspect of this exciting game!

**NUMBER OF PLAYERS:** 2 players (additional players can play in pairs)

**SUGGESTED AGE LEVEL:** 6-12 years of age

**EQUIPMENT:** 1 beanbag (or any small object)

**HOW TO PLAY:** Have the two players stand facing each other with the beanbag on the ground between them. A safety line is marked about 30 feet behind each player.

The game begins with the players exchanging a handshake. This is done after each turn to prevent players from starting too early. After the handshake, the players can grab the beanbag at any time. The objective is to steal the beanbag and make it back to the safety line without getting tagged (resulting in a point), or if the other player grabs the beanbag first, tagging him before he reaches his safety line (resulting in a point for the tagger). After each turn, the players return to the middle, place the beanbag on the ground, shake hands, and begin play again.

As a safety precaution when grabbing for the beanbag, remind the players to keep their eyes up and not to put their head down. In addition, instruct the players to move to their left each time upon grabbing the beanbag (therefore going in opposite directions). These actions will help prevent collisions.

150

# ROCK PAPER SCISSORS
## (One-On-One)

**INTRODUCTION & PURPOSE:** This one-on-one activity is a modification of the game *Rock, Paper, Scissors*. In that game, players are stationary and it's mainly used as a way to settle a dispute, decide who is going to go first, who will be "It," etc. This game provides all the suspense of regular *Rock, Paper, Scissors,* but with chasing and fleeing added to provide lots of healthy movement.

**NUMBER OF PLAYERS:** 2 players (additional players can play in pairs)

**SUGGESTED AGE LEVEL:** 7-13 years of age

**EQUIPMENT:** None

**HOW TO PLAY:** Have two players stand facing each other in the middle of two safety lines which are marked about 30 feet behind each player.

The game begins with the two players performing a rock, paper, scissors. A rock is a closed fist, paper is a flat hand, and scissors are the index and middle fingers in a cutting position. Paper covers rock, rock breaks scissors, and scissors cut paper. To determine a winner, the players count to three and at the same time (on three) form a rock, paper, or scissors. The winning player then chases the losing player toward his safety line and attempts to tag him before reaching the line. If successful, the chaser is credited with a point. No point is awarded if the runner makes it back untagged to his safety line. After each turn, the players return to the middle and play again. Throughout the game, only the winner of the Rock, Paper, Scissors contest can chase and score points.

Players can keep score if they like. However, most children will find that it's not necessary. As with other tag games, they'll probably want to play just for the fun of chasing and fleeing from each other.

# RED LIGHT

**INTRODUCTION & PURPOSE:** *Red Light* is a variation of the classic game of Red Light, Green Light. Traditionally, this game is played in a large group setting, but the author's experience has shown that it can be successfully played with as few as three players. In fact, the smaller number makes it a success-oriented (and inclusive) activity for children.

Game leaders can change the type of movement skills used throughout the game so children are developing a wider range of skills besides running (normally the only movement used in Red Light, Green Light).

**NUMBER OF PLAYERS:** 3 or more players

**SUGGESTED AGE LEVEL:** 6-9 years of age

**EQUIPMENT:** None

**HOW TO PLAY:** Select one player to be the "Traffic Light." The Traffic Light stands on a line about 40 feet from the other players.

The object of this game is to move across the playing area successfully without getting caught by the Traffic Light player. The game begins with the Traffic Light player turning his back to the line players and calling out "green light." The line players move toward the Traffic Light in a movement specified by the game leader (skipping, galloping, running, etc.). However, at any time, the Traffic Light can call out "red light," which signals that the line players must come to an immediate stop. Any player caught moving by the Traffic Light must go back to the starting line for the next turn. Players who successfully come to a stop are allowed to stay where they are. Play continues in this fashion until one of the players touches the Traffic Light. This player becomes the Traffic Light for the next round of play.

To give players enough time to come to a stop on a "red light," the Traffic Light player might need to clap his hands three times before turning around.

152

# SCURRYING SQUIRRELS

**INTRODUCTION & PURPOSE:** This exciting activity improves fundamental motor skills and develops cardiovascular fitness. *Scurrying Squirrels* can be played with 3 players, but it's more challenging with 4 players. This is a great choice as a closing activity in a physical education lesson.

**NUMBER OF PLAYERS:** 3-4 players to a game (set up additional playing areas for larger groups)

**SUGGESTED AGE LEVEL:** 8-14 years of age

**EQUIPMENT:** 5 hoops (or 4 hoops for 3 players), 8 beanbags

**HOW TO PLAY:** Arrange five hoops as shown in the diagram. Place the eight beanbags (acorns) in the middle hoop. A player (squirrel) is to stand in each of the four outside hoops.

The objective is to be the first player with three "acorns" in his hoop. On a starting signal, each player runs to the middle hoop, takes one beanbag and places it inside his hoop. The players repeat this again until they each have two beanbags resting inside their hoops. At this point, players can steal beanbags from each other's hoops. Because no player can defend the beanbags in his hoop, there is always a place from which to steal a beanbag. A player can take only one beanbag at a time.

Game leaders may want to teach that defensive strategy is important to winning in this game. Although a player can't defend his own hoop, he can try to take the beanbags away from a player closest to winning.

Consider adding additional "acorns" in the middle hoop if a game gets too easy.

# TAG GAMES

**INTRODUCTION & PURPOSE:** Tag games are often the most played playground activities by children. The reason for this is simple–they're fun!

Tag games, with their high level of movement, are not only appropriate recess activities, they're also terrific warm-ups for the physical education class. Simple and well-known rules allow tag activities to be set up quickly, avoiding lengthy periods of explanation. All of the tag games described below require participation by everyone, and they avoid exclusionary rules (which result in children having to sit out). Homeschooling families will also appreciate how these games can be played in a variety of settings, and require only a few participants.

**NUMBER OF PLAYERS:** Most of the games described below require only several players.

**SUGGESTED AGE LEVEL:** Although tag games are often associated with young children, individuals of varying abilities and ages will benefit from the healthy exercise and challenging fun provided by these games of pursuit.

**EQUIPMENT:** Most of the tag games described below require some kind of identification for the chaser(s). Read the game description for the equipment needs of a particular game.

**HOW TO PLAY:** Before playing any tag game, children need to be instructed on how to travel safely in a group setting. Encourage jogging or walking instead of running, particularly for the 6-8 year olds. Eyes should always be focused forward. Avoid playing in areas in which dangerous objects exists that players could collide with.

Follow the specific directions and rules for each game.

## BRIDGE TAG

Depending on the number of players, select 1 or 2 chasers. The chasers are given pinnies (colored jerseys) for identification. When a player is tagged, he makes a bridge by going down on his hands and feet. A tagged player must stay in this position until a free player crawls through his bridge. This is a continuous action game that doesn't end unless all the players are frozen or time has been called.

## CIRCLE TAG

This game requires four players. Three players join hands to make a circle. One player stands outside the circle and is the tagger. The tagger names one of the circle players that he will attempt to touch. The tagger has to move around the outside of the circle to touch the named player. He can not reach across the middle.

The circle players can not run around the playing area, but they can move either clockwise or counterclockwise to help the player from being tagged. Once the tagger is successful, he switches place with the tagged player and joins the circle. Play continues again with the new tagger calling out the name of the next player to be chased.

# FIRST AID TAG

Designate 1 or 2 players to start as the chasers, each holding a small foam ball for identification. When a player is tagged, he has to put a hand on the spot (his "injury") where he was touched, and he continues playing. When touched a second time, he puts his other hand on the spot where he was touched and now continues playing with each hand on his "injuries." When tagged a third time, he takes a foam ball and becomes a tagger himself. The game ends when all players have become taggers.

# FREEZE TAG

Choose 1-2 players to be taggers ("freezers") and 1 or 2 players ("defrosters") to free others. The taggers attempt to freeze all the players whom, after being tagged, stand in a motionless position. At the same time, the defrosters move around touching the frozen players which allows them to become free. The defrosters have to avoid the taggers as they can become frozen as well. Play continues until all the players are frozen or time is called.

# FUNNY FACE TAG

Select 1 or 2 chasers, each wearing an identification pinnie. On a starting signal, the taggers attempt to tag as players as possible. Once tagged, a player puts his hands on his hips and stands with a sad look on his face. However, he can play again if a free player comes up to him with a "funny face,' which makes him laugh or smile. Play is continuous and doesn't end unless all the players have been tagged or time has been called.

# GERM TAG

Start with 1 or 2 players each holding a foam ball (the "germ"). On a starting signal, each of the chasers attempt to tag another player. A tagged player takes the ball and becomes the new tagger. The newly tagged player now quickly tries to tag another player so he is not stuck with the "germ" for very long. The game objective is to avoid getting getting tagged and becoming a chaser. Play until time is called.

# GOTCHA

Each player starts with one beanbag. The object of the game is to tag others by underhand throwing the beanbag at the feet of the other players, and to avoid being tagged by others. Once a player has a beanbag hit his foot, he must do 5 jumping jacks (or any similar exercise) at that spot before rejoining the game. Play is continuous until time is called.

# HIGH FIVE TAG

Select 1 or 2 players to be the chasers. Each chaser should have an identification pinnie. When players are tagged, they freeze motionless with one hand high in the air. A tagged player rejoins the game once someone gives him a high five. The game is continuous until time is called.

# JUMPING JACK TAG

Choose 1 or 2 players to start as the chasers. Each chaser needs to wear a pinnie so they can be distinguished from the others. Because there are no safe bases or walls, if players want to stop running and not be tagged, they must do jumping jacks (or a similar exercise such as push-ups, sit-ups, etc.). Tagged players trade places with the chasers who tagged them. Play is continuous until time is called.

# LEAPFROG TAG

Choose 1 or 2 players to begin as taggers, each wearing a pinnie for identification.. When players are tagged, they crouch in a leapfrog position. A tagged player is rescued and returns to the game when someone leapfrogs over them. The game is continuous until all the players are tagged or until time is called.

# LINE TAG

This game is best played on a lined basketball court (either indoors or outdoors). Have the players stand anywhere on a black line. Select 1 or 2 players to be chasers, each holding a small foam ball for identification. On a starting signal, the taggers chase the players attempting to touch another player with his ball. No throwing is allowed. Once a player is tagged, he takes the ball and becomes the new tagger. All players, including the taggers, must travel on the lines. Play is continuous until time is called.

# PARTNER TAG

Everyone pairs up with a partner. One player in each pair begins as the tagger and holds a beanbag. On a starting signal, the tagger attempts to touch his partner with the beanbag. No throwing is allowed. Once a partner is tagged, he takes the beanbag and spins in a circle twice before pursuing the other player. Play is continuous until time is called.

On a cautionary note, this game needs to be restricted to two players, or if more than one pair of players are playing, require walking instead of running. Otherwise, players could run into each other resulting in an injury.

# SPORTS TAG

Select 1 or 2 players to begin as chasers, each holding a small foam ball for identification. Chasers must touch, and cannot throw the ball at others while pursuing them. A tagged player assumes a statue depicting a sports player. For example, this might be a baseball in a batting stance, a basketball player shooting, a golfer in a swinging position, etc. A tagged player can rejoin the game when another player comes up to him and correctly calls out name of the sport he is depicting. If a player remains in a statue position after two guesses, he can give verbal clues to players attempting to free him. Play is continuous until time is called.

# STUCK IN THE MUD

Designate one or two players to start as the chasers, each wearing a pinnie for identification. The taggers attempt to tag everyone in order to end the game. Tagged players stand motionless with their feet apart, hands on top of their heads. A tagged player is free when another player crawls between his legs. Play is continuous until time is called.

# TUNNEL TAG

Choose 1 or 2 players to begin as the chasers, each wearing a pinnie for identification. Tagged players must make a tunnel and remain in that position until another player crawls through it allowing him to play again. Tunnel examples include a player on all fours, an upside down tunnel on all fours, a standing tunnel with the feet apart, a wall tunnel with the feet on a wall supported by the hands on the floor, etc. Play is continuous until time is called.

# TRUE OR FALSE
## (One-On-One)

**INTRODUCTION OR PURPOSE:** This is another game that is traditionally played with a large group. To meet the needs of the homeschooling family, as well as to make it an inclusive learning experience (even for larger groups of children), the participant format has been changed to that of a one-on-one activity. This game combines the review of academic concepts with the fun and excitement of a chasing and fleeing game.

**NUMBER OF PLAYERS:** 2 players (although larger groups can be paired up for additional one-on-one games)

**SUGGESTED AGE LEVEL:** 6-14 years of age

**EQUIPMENT:** None

**HOW TO PLAY:** Have two players stand facing each other in the middle of two safety lines which are marked about 30 feet behind each player. Designate one player as the "True" player, and the other as "False."

The game begins with the game leader calling out a statement that is unmistakably true or false. The game leader can use math problems (such as 10 multiplied by 10 equals...), word spelling, geography facts, etc. If the statement is true, the "True" player chases the "False" player back to his safety line attempting to tag him. If the statement is false, the "False" player chases the "True" player. A point is awarded to the chasing player if he successfully tags the fleeing player. Likewise, a point is awarded to the fleeing player if he successfully makes back to the safety line without being tagged. After each turn, the players return to the middle and play again.

**VARIATIONS:** A couple of variations using academic themes are described below. The set-up and format of the games are the same as in *True Or False*. Again, these games are wonderful tools for integrating academic subjects into the physical education class.

# VOWELS & CONSONANTS

This variation provides an opportunity to link language arts and physical education. Designate one child as the "Vowel" player, and the other as the "Consonant." The game leader calls out a letter. If a vowel is called, such as "e," the vowel player runs to his safety line with the consonant player in pursuit. Likewise, if a consonant is called, such as "n," the consonant player runs toward his safety line with the vowel player in pursuit. Scoring is the same as in *True Or False*. After each turn, the players return to the middle and play again.

# STATES & CAPITOLS

This variation provides an opportunity to link geography and physical education. Designate one child as the "States," and the other as the "Capitols" player. The game leader calls out either the name of a state, such as Oregon, or the name of a Capitol, such as Salem. If a state is called, the state player chases the capitol player toward his safety line attempting to tag him. Likewise, if a capitol is called, the capitol player runs toward his safety line with the states player in pursuit. Scoring is the same as in *True Or False*. After each turn, the players return to the middle and play again.

# ULTIMATE

**INTRODUCTION & PURPOSE:** *Ultimate* is a modification of the large-group game *Ultimate Frisbee*. This version allows a frisbee, but it also allows any type of object or ball to be used for throwing and catching. In fact, children will benefit from playing this game with a variety of objects, such as a football, whiffle ball, foam ball, etc.

**NUMBER OF PLAYERS:** 4 players (although up to 3-4 players on a team would still result in an inclusive-style play experience)

**SUGGESTED AGE LEVEL:** 9-17 years of age

**EQUIPMENT:** 1 object for throwing (a frisbee, football or similar ball), cones

**HOW TO PLAY:** Mark off a playing area that is approximately 35-60 feet wide and 50-90 feet long. The actual distance can vary depending on the age and skill level of the players. Each team stands on opposite end lines, with one team starting on offense with the ball.

The offensive team begins the game by advancing the ball down the field by throwing and catching to each other. Players in possession of the ball cannot walk or run with it. However, they can pivot on one foot (as in basketball) while trying to pass. A "traveling" violation results in the other team taking possession of the ball at the spot of the infraction.

The defensive team can intercept, or knock away the ball at any time. Additionally, any thrown ball that falls uncaught to the ground results in the defensive team taking possession at that spot. Defensive players can guard but cannot touch or make any physical contact with an offensive player. A "roughing" violation results in a free, unguarded throw.

To score, the offensive team must have the ball caught by a teammate behind the opponent's end line. Each score counts as 1 point. After each score, the teams line up again on their end lines with the non-scoring team starting with possession of the ball. Play continues until a team has reached a predetermined number of points, or a time limit has expired.

# Section 9

# FITNESS-BUILDING GAMES

Fitness-building games are just what the name implies, activities full of challenging fun that enhance strength and/or cardiovascular endurance. The activities included in this chapter focus on maximum participation, which provides for the best play and fitness enhancing experience for children. The idea for parents and game leaders is not to have the children focus on the "wins," but rather on the opportunities for personal challenge in a fun and relaxed setting.

# BEAN BAG FITNESS CHALLENGES

**INTRODUCTION & PURPOSE:**  The one-on-one activities described below are ideal introductory and closing activities for the physical education lesson. These games are quick to set up and explain (important qualities for introductory and closing activities), they're packed with challenging fun, and they'll benefit children of all ages.

**NUMBER OF PLAYERS:**  2 players to a group; an unlimited number of groups can play simultaneously

**SUGGESTED AGE LEVEL:** 7-17 years of age

**EQUIPMENT:**  1 beanbag for each pair of players

**HOW TO PLAY:**  Pair up players so each has a partner. As with all partner challenges, game leaders should pair up players of equal size and skill as much as possible. Specific directions for each game are explained below.

## PUSH-UP HOCKEY

This activity builds upper body strength, endurance, body control, and improves movement reaction time.

Two players begin by facing each other about 3 feet to 5 feet apart in the up position of a push–up position. One player is given a beanbag, and he starts the game by trying to quickly slide it through the opponent's arms (the hockey goal). The opponent can block the beanbag with a hand or arm. Players take alternate turns after each attempt. A point is awarded each time to the player who successfully slides the beanbag through the arms.

Because of the need for a sliding beanbag (it can not be thrown in the air), it's best to play this game indoors on a tile or wood surface.

# STEAL THE BEANS (sitting)

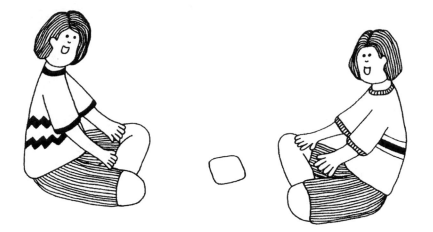

Although this activity doesn't build strength or endurance, it's a fun "breather" in-between the other more physically demanding activities listed in this chapter. It also develops listening and reaction time skills.

Partners sit in a cross-legged position facing each other. A beanbag is placed on the floor directly in the middle of the partners. If you have three players, the extra player can play by forming a triangle and placing the beanbag in the middle of the three players.

The game leader begins by calling out "ready," which informs the players that they need to place their hands on their thighs. At any time, the game leader then calls out "right" or "left." The players react quickly by reaching for the beanbag with the hand that was called. A point is awarded to the player who first grabs the beanbag. The beanbag is placed back in the middle after each turn.

# STEAL THE BEANS (push-up)

This game develops upper body fitness, endurance, body control, listening, and reaction skills. The game is played exactly like Sitting Steal The Beans (see game description above) with one exception–players are now in the up position of a push-up. Scoring is the same as in Sitting Steal The Beans. The contest ends after a predetermined number of points.

# OVER THE BACK RELAY

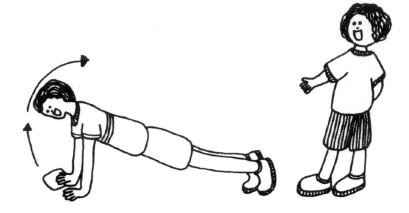

This activity develops upper body strength, cardiovascular endurance, balance, body control, and catching skills. The game can be played as a cooperative activity in which the objective is for the partners to successfully finish the course. For competitive play, the players can be paired into relay teams with the objective of finishing the course first.

One player begins in the up position of a push-up, holding a beanbag. The partner stands behind him. On a starting signal, the player in the push-up position tosses the beanbag over his shoulders high into the air so his partner can catch it. If the receiver catches it, he runs around the thrower and immediately goes down in a push-up position. The push-up player stands up and now becomes the next receiver. The players continue this alternating pattern until they reach the finishing line.

# BEANBAG FOOT TAG

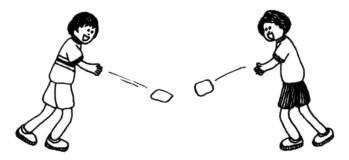

This game can be played with a partner (one-on-one), or as a group activity (everyone against everyone). Cardiovascular endurance, body control, agility, and throwing skills are all enhanced by this activity.

Each player starts with one beanbag. The object of the game is to tag the partner (or others) by underhand throwing the beanbag at the feet of the opponent, and at the same time, avoid being tagged. A player is awarded a point for each successful tag. Play continues until one player has reached a predetermined number of points.

# CLEAN UP YOUR TRASH

**INTRODUCTION & PURPOSE:** This game is patterned after a favorite large-group game called *Clean Up The Trash*. In that game, players throw balls in order to have a "cleaner house." There is no throwing in this version, but the player's goal of having no trash (the beanbags) in their house (the hoop) is similar. This game provides lots of cardiovascular fitness fun!

**NUMBER OF PLAYERS:** 3 players or more

**SUGGESTED AGE LEVEL:** 8-14 years of age

**EQUIPMENT:** 2 beanbags and 1 hoop for each player

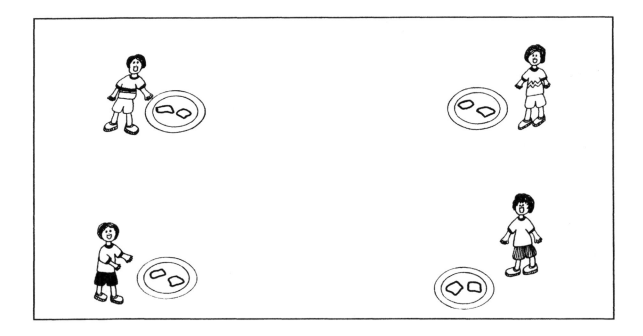

**HOW TO PLAY:** Arrange the hoops to form four corners of a square with each side about 20 feet long (see diagram). One player is to stand in each hoop (a "house"). Two beanbags (the "trash") are placed on the ground inside each hoop.

Each player's goal is to get rid of his two beanbags, one at a time, by depositing them into other's hoops. On the start signal, each player grabs one beanbag, runs to an opponent's hoop and places it on the ground inside that hoop. They then run back to their hoop and repeat the same process again. They keep doing this until one player has no trash (beanbags) in his house (hoop).

A player can not defend his hoop by preventing a player from placing a beanbag inside his hoop. However, he can strategically place one of his beanbags into an opponent's hoop if he notices that player is close to winning.

Consider adding a beanbag to each hoop, so that each player starts with three, if the game is too easy.

# PARTNER BALL RELAYS

**INTRODUCTION & PURPOSE:** *Partner Ball Relays* are not only fun, they're also great for developing physical fitness, agility, and cooperation. Game leaders can use these activities in a competitive format in which the players attempt to finish the relay as quickly as possible, or as a non-competitive event in which the objective is for the partners to simply accomplish the task at their own pace.

**NUMBER OF PLAYERS:** 2 players per team; unlimited teams

**SUGGESTED AGE LEVEL:** 8-14 years of age

**EQUIPMENT:** 1 large playground ball for each pair of students

**HOW TO PLAY:** Mark off starting and finishing lines that are approximately 30 feet apart. This distance can vary depending on the age of the players. Assign each player a partner, and give each pair a playground ball.

The objective is to carry the playground ball to the finishing line without touching each other or the ball with the hands. There are a variety of challenges that can be presented to the players. These include having partners travel with the ball squeezed between the shoulders, the hips, the heads, bottoms, backs, elbows, etc.

There is no limit to the number of drops a team can make. If playing competitively, the objective is to be the first team to cross the finish line.

# MISCELLANEOUS
# PARTNER CHALLENGES

**INTRODUCTION & PURPOSE:** These fitness-building activities are wonderful introductory and closing activities for a physical education lesson. They are quick to explain, easy to understand, require no equipment, appropriate for all ages, and they're packed with fun.

**NUMBER OF PLAYERS:** 2 players to a group; unlimited groups can play simultaneously

**SUGGESTED AGE LEVEL:** 7-17 years of age

**EQUIPMENT:** None

**HOW TO PLAY:** All of the games require a partner. Specific directions for each game are explained below.

## KING OF THE MOUNTAIN

Mark a circle ("mountain") that is about 9-10 feet in diameter. Partners stand back-to-back in the middle. On a starting signal, the players push backwards using only their feet. The objective is to push the opponent out of the circle. After each turn, players return to the middle and play again. Remind the players to not use their elbows and to keep their backs in contact with each other throughout the contest.

# CRAB GRAB

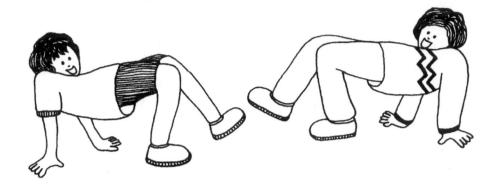

The players begin in a "crab" position (see illustration above). On a signal, the players use their feet and hands to force the opponent's bottom to touch the floor. If successful, a player is awarded a point. After each turn, the players return to their starting position and resume play. Players are not allowed to kick or punch. Instead, players are to use only grab and pull type movements.

# FAKE & PUSH

In Fake & Push, the objective is to make your opponent lose balance without moving your own feet. Players begin by facing each other, about 2 to 3 feet apart, with the palms of both hands against each other. Players must stand with their feet together. Each player attempts to make his partner lose his balance by pushing, dodging, or feinting. Moving a foot, no matter how slightly, signifies a loss of balance. A point is awarded to the player that is successful at causing the loss of balance. After each turn, players return to their starting positions and resume play.

Once the game starts the palms do not need to stay together. Moving the hands out of the way when the other player is pushing may result in the pusher's momentum carrying him off balance. This strategy of feinting is often the key to winning.

# KNEE BOXING

No, boxing is not allowed. However, the circling, feinting, and quick movements might lead some to think that they are. The partners begin by facing each in a crouched position. On a signal, each player attempts to touch the opponent's knee with an open hand. Each time a knee is touched, the player earns one point. Play continues until one player has received 10 points. Players are not allowed to tackle, trip, or hang on an opponent–touching the knee is only kind of touch allowed.

# BEAR TAG

Mark off a circle that is about 8 to 10 feet in diameter. The two players start by facing each other in a "bear" position (on all fours) with a flag hanging from the back of their belt or back pocket. The objective is to "tag" the opponent by pulling his flag. The game begins with the two players circling and making a variety of quick movements to position themselves for a pull of the opponent's flag. Players are to stay inside the circle, and have to stay in a bear position as much as possible. Also, no wrestling, kicking, or any other form of rough play is allowed. A player who is successful at pulling the opponent's flag is awarded one point. After each turn, players return to their starting positions and resume play.

# PUSH-UP TAG

The two players start by facing each other in the up position of a push-up. The objective is to make more touches on the opponent's hands than he makes on your hands. The game begins with the players attempting to tag either hand of the opponent, and at the same time, avoiding getting tagged. Players can use a variety of circling and feinting movements before going for a quick touch. A successful tag counts as one point. Play continues until one player reaches a predetermined number of points. Players must remain in a push-up position throughout the game.

# TOE BOXING

Like Knee Boxing, there is no actual boxing in this game—however, the title is sure to catch the attention of children! Toe Boxing is a great energizer that can be used at any time during the physical education lesson.

Players face each other with their hands placed on the shoulders of their partner. Using their feet, each player tries to touch the toes of the other player. Each successful touch counts as a point. The first player to receive 10 points wins the contest.

Players can circle and make feinting movements in order to make a quick touch. However, players must keep their hands on the opponent's shoulders at all times.

# ROPELESS TUG O' WAR

**INTRODUCTION & PURPOSE:** Your children want to play tug o' war but they don't have a rope? *Ropeless Tug o' War* is the answer to this dilemma! This strength-building activity can be played in any setting, is quick to set up and explain, and it only requires a minimum of two players on a team.

**NUMBER OF PLAYERS:** 4 or more players

**SUGGESTED AGE LEVEL:** 7-17 years of age

**EQUIPMENT:** None

**HOW TO PLAY:** Two teams stand in a single-file line with each player grasping the waist of the player in front. The first player reaches across the center line to grasp the hands of the other team's first player (see illustration above).

On a starting signal, each team begins pulling in an attempt to pull the other team entirely across the center line for the win. Players must be grasping the player in front during the entire duration of the pull.

As with any type of tug o' war contest, game leaders should review with the players the potential hazards of landing backwards. Players should learn to anticipate the fall and use the hands to soften the landing.

**VARIATION:** Two players can play a one-on-one version of *Ropeless Tug O' War* by simply following the same format as above but without the extra players.

# ROPE JOUSTING

**INTRODUCTION & PURPOSE:** *Rope Jousting* is actually a modification of an early American game called Rooks. At that time, players would stand on sawed-off stumps in a water or mud setting with the goal of not being pulled off the stump. No need for that now—hula hoops work great! This strength-building activity will be enjoyed by children of all ages.

**NUMBER OF PLAYERS:** 2 players

**SUGGESTED AGE LEVEL:** 6-17 years of age

**EQUIPMENT:** 2 hoops, 1 long jump rope (about 12-16 feet in length)

**HOW TO PLAY:** Place two hoops about 10 feet apart, with a player in each hoop. The two players start by holding the end of the rope.

The objective is to unbalance the opponent so that he falls out of his hoop. On a starting signal, the two players begin pulling, as well as letting the rope slip a little, so that the other player steps out of his hoop (with at least one foot).

Unlike regular tug o' war, strength is not the only factor to winning. Keeping one's balance during the opponent's rope slips is a strategy that players should be aware of. (Special note: no player is allowed to totally release the rope.)

Game leaders might want to initially play this game outdoors. This will lessen any anxiety that players might have in falling out of a hoop. Additionally, the hoops tend to move around less on grass versus a floor with a tile or wood surface.

# FITNESS FRISBEE

**INTRODUCTION & PURPOSE:** *Fitness Frisbee* is designed to improve the cardiovascular fitness of children in a nontraditional way. Some children might not like the idea of running for fitness enhancement. However, by combining a fun activity such as frisbee throwing with the distance running, you create a fitness-oriented activity that is more enjoyable for children.

**NUMBER OF PLAYERS:** 2 or more

**SUGGESTED AGE LEVEL:** 6-17 years of age

**EQUIPMENT:** 1 frisbee for each player

**HOW TO PLAY:** This cross country running/frisbee throwing activity can be played in a variety of ways, but the overall objective for each player is the same—finish the course with the least amount of throws. First, lay out a cross-country course. For younger children, the distance can be across a field or playground and back. For older players, it may be a mile loop or longer. On a starting signal, each player tosses his frisbee, runs to pick it up, throws it again, etc., until he has covered a certain distance and returned to the starting line. The objective is to cover the distance in as few throws as possible.

**VARIATION:** Consider having a series of targets that a player must hit with his frisbee while running the course. The objective of finishing the course in the least amount of throws remains the same as above.

Another variation is to conduct the game as a race with an objective of being the first player back to the finish line regardless of the number of throws. If using this variation, implement a rule in which the players cannot run with a frisbee in hand.

# Section 10

# ROPE JUMPING ACTIVITIES

**Rope jumping is one of the most beneficial physical education activities children can participate in. It involves skills that are simple enough for six-year olds to master, as well as steps that are challenging even for an adult athlete. It requires little space, is relatively inexpensive, is suitable for both boys and girls, and most importantly–it's fun! Included in this chapter are teaching strategies and challenges for both long and individual rope jumping.**

# LONG ROPE JUMPING

**INTRODUCTION & PURPOSE:** Long rope jumping is an excellent activity for beginning jumpers, as they can concentrate on jumping the rope before learning the skill of turning. However, older children will also find long rope jumping an enjoyable experience and will be challenged in performing some of the advanced steps.

The many physical benefits of rope jumping include the development of cardiovascular endurance, strength development, agility, body control, and increased hand-eye-foot coordination. Long rope jumping also enhances social growth and group cooperation as it necessitates several players working together to accomplish a common goal.

**NUMBER OF PLAYERS:** 3 players to a rope

**SUGGESTED AGE LEVEL:** 6-17 years of age

**EQUIPMENT:** 1 long jump rope (10 to 12 feet long for the younger children; 14 to 16 feet long for the older children)

**HOW TO PLAY:** The proper execution of turning a rope is critical to successful jumping. If turning is not rhythmic, even skilled jumpers will have problems. However, turning the rope is a difficult skill for young children, and it should be practiced regularly until an even, steady rhythm is developed. While the skill of turning is practiced on its own, the younger children can still participate in the non-turning jumps, such as Jump The Stick, High Water, Pendulum Jump, etc.

The following instructional procedures are essential when introducing beginning turning and jumping skills with the long ropes.

1. When teaching children how to turn, emphasize keeping the elbow close to the body and concentrate on turning the rope with the forearm. Lock the wrist and keep the thumb up while turning. The rope should barely touch the floor each time.

176

2. A good swing for the rope turners to use at the start of a turn is called the "blue bell" technique. That is, three pendulum swings (half swings) are followed by a full turn.
3. Beginning jumpers should concentrate on mastering the stationary jump (see Jump The Stick) and half-swing jumps (see Pendulum Jump) before attempting to jump with a full turn.
4. Introduce the terms *Front Door* and *Back Door* when children are ready to start entering a turning rope. *Front Door* means entering from the side where the rope is turning forward and toward the jumper after it reaches its peak. To enter front door, the jumper follows the rope in and jumps when it completes the turn. *Back Door* means entering from the side where the rope is turning backward and away from the jumper. To enter back door, the jumper waits until the rope reaches its peak and moves in as the rope moves downward.

The following are jumps that you can have children perform. In order, they progress from the less difficult jumps to the more challenging tasks.

## JUMP THE STICK

The turners hold the rope completely motionless, with the middle about 6 inches off the floor. The jumper stands in the middle facing one of the turners. The jumper begins by jumping sideways back and forth over the rope, completely clearing it each time. After 10 consecutive jumps, the players rotate with a turner becoming the next jumper. After the initial turn, jumpers should try jumping forward and backward 10 times (not sideways).

## HIGH WATER

This jump adds a little challenge to Jump The Stick. One rope turner holds the motionless rope waist level high, and the other turner holds his end to the floor. Starting at the low end, the jumper progresses up the rope, jumping higher and higher as he approaches the high end of the rope. Players rotate positions after each turn.

## PENDULUM JUMP

This jump is named after the style of rope swing that resembles the pendulum on a grandfather's clock. The turners swing the rope back and forth (half turns). Jumpers can either start in the middle or they can enter a moving rope. Players rotate positions after each turn.

## RUN THROUGH

The turners execute the regular full turn swing. Players take turns running through the turning rope without getting touched. Both the *Front Door* and *Back Door* entries can be introduced and performed with this activity.

# REGULAR JUMPING

Jumpers attempt to jump a turning rope a predetermined number of times. Begin with the jumper in the middle, and progress to having the jumpers enter a turning rope.

# JUMP STUNTS

After the players have mastered regular jumping, consider adding some challenges such as performing quarter and half turns, touching the ground after each jump, straddle jumping, using a rocker step, etc. Also consider using challenges with equipment, such as bouncing a ball while jumping, jumping a hula hoop (like a short rope) while jumping the long rope, juggling while jumping, etc.

# HOT PEPPER

With a jumper in the middle, the turners begin by turning the rope slowly. They progressively turn it faster and faster. The objective for the jumper is to last as long as possible.

# THE RISING BRIDGE

With a jumper in the middle, the turners begin by turning the rope slowly. After several turns of the rope, one of the turners (not both) gradually walks backward causing the middle of the rope to rise higher. The jumper must jump progressively higher and higher to avoid stopping the rope.

# EGG BEATER

This challenging jump requires five players (four turners and one jumper), and two ropes. The ropes are crossed in a "+" pattern, with each end held by a turner. In unison, both ropes are turned either front door or back door. The jumper attempts to enter the turning ropes, jump a predetermined number of times, and exit without stopping the ropes.

# DOUBLE DUTCH

This type of jumping requires two rope turners turning the ropes in opposite directions. Turners rotate the hands inward toward middle of the body with the right forearm moving counterclockwise and the left forearm clockwise. Jumpers enter by standing beside a turner and running into the ropes when the back rope (farther from the jumper) touches the floor.

178

# INDIVIDUAL ROPE JUMPING

**INTRODUCTION & PURPOSE:** After children understand the rhythmical jumping required with a long rope, they usually progress rather easily to an individual rope. As with the long rope, jumping with an individual rope is packed with fitness and skill benefits. It's particularly valuable as part of the conditioning component of a physical education lesson.

**NUMBER OF PLAYERS:** 1 player for each rope; an unlimited number of jumpers can participate simultaneously if space permits

**SUGGESTED AGE LEVEL:** 6-17 years of age

**EQUIPMENT:** 1 rope for each player (rope lengths can vary from 5 feet for the youngest children to 9 feet for the older children)

**HOW TO PLAY:** Each child needs one rope. The length of the rope is dependent on the height of the jumper. It should be long enough so the ends reach the armpits or slightly higher when the child stands on its center.

When children experience difficulty in jumping, it is usually a problem in the coordination of hand and foot movements. Remember that rope jumping involves two separate skills: jumping a rope and turning a rope. Without a rope, let them practice a "pretend" jump. That is, they move the hands and practice jumping with correct rhythm and footwork. The next progression would be to hold the rope to one side with both hands, swing the rope forward and jump each time the rope hits the floor. Finally, have them progress to jumping forward and backward over a stationary rope that they hold in front of them. Gradually increase the swing until a full turn of the rope is made.

Some instructional procedures to use for improving jumping technique are as follows:
1. The body should be in good alignment, with the head up and the eyes looking straight ahead. The jump is made with the body in an erect position.

2. The rope should be held by the index finger and thumb on each side, with the elbows held near the sides of the body.
3. While turning, keep the arms at the side of the body. Many children mistakenly lift the arms trying to move the rope overhead. This makes it impossible to jump over the elevated rope.
4. Turn the rope by making small circles with the wrists.
5. The landing should be made on the balls of the feet, with the knees bent slightly to cushion the force of the jump.
6. Introduce the terms *Slow Time* and *Fast Time* when the children are ready to jump with a turn of the rope. In slow time rhythm, the player jumps over the rope, rebounds, and then executes the second jump. The rebound is simply a hop in place as the rope passes over the head. The result is two jumps for each turn. In fast time rhythm, the player jumps one time for each turn of the rope.

The following are basic jump steps. In order, they are listed from the least difficult to the more challenging.

# TWO FOOT JUMP

This is often the first step children learn when introduced to the individual rope. Using either fast or slow time rhythm (see above), the player jumps over the rope with both feet together.

# ALTERNATE FOOT STEP

In the Alternate Foot Step, the jumper alternately shifts his feet as the rope passes under the feet, resembling a running-in-place pattern.

# DOUBLE SIDE SWING JUMP

Swing the rope once on each side of the body. Follow the second swing with a jump over the rope. Repeat the swing, swing, jump pattern.

# BIRD JUMPS

Similar to the Two Foot Jump, except the player alternately jumps with the toes pointed in (as in a pigeon walk) and with the toes pointed out (as in a duck walk). Repeat the toes in, toes out pattern.

# ROCKER STEP

In performing this step, one leg is always forward in a walking-stride position. As the rope passes under the front foot, the weight is shifted from the back foot to the forward foot. Shift the weight from the front foot to the back foot after the rope passes underneath. The motion resembles that of a rocking chair going back and forth.

## STRADDLE JUMP

The jumper alternates a regular jump with a straddle jump. The straddle jump is performed with the feet spread to shoulder width. After the straddle jump, the performer moves his feet back together. The motion resembles a jumping jack exercise.

## MOUNTAIN CLIMBER

Start in a stride position (as in the Rocker) with one leg in front of the other. The weight should be equally distributed on both feet. As the rope passes under the feet, jump into the air and reverse the position of the feet.

## MOUNTAIN SKIER

The performer jumps sideways, off both feet, over a line on the floor. The sideways motion resembles that of a skier moving down a mountain slope. Children should try it in a forward and backward direction also.

## CROSS LEGS JUMP

The performer begins by jumping off both feet and taking the rebound in a straddle position. As the rope passes under the feet on the next turn, jump into the air and cross the feet with the right foot forward. Then repeat with the left foot forward and continue this alternation.

## SHUFFLE STEP

This resembles a dance step as it involves pushing off with the right foot and sidestepping to the left as the rope passes under the feet. Land with the weight on the left foot and touch the right toes beside the left heel. Repeat the step in the opposite direction.

## HEEL-TOE STEP

As the rope passes under the feet, jump with the weight landing on the left foot while touching the right heel forward. On the next turn of the rope, jump, land on the same foot, and touch the right toes beside the left heel. Repeat the pattern with the opposite foot bearing the weight.

## SKIPPING STEP

The jumper performs a step-hop (skip) as the rope passes under the feet.

## BLEKING STEP

The step begins with a hop on the left foot with the right heel forward, followed by a hop on the right with the left heel forward. This action is repeated with a slow-slow, fast-fast-fast pattern.

## CRISS-CROSS JUMP

Start with the feet together. As the rope is turning overhead, cross the arms in front of the body to create a loop with the rope. The arms stay crossed as the player jumps through the loop. As the rope passes under the feet, the player uncrosses the arms and performs a regular two-foot jump. Repeat the alternating pattern.

## DOUBLE UNDERS

The jumper starts with a few basic two-foot jumps in preparation for the double turn. As the rope approaches the feet, the player turns the rope with a fast whip from the wrists, jumps from 4-8 inches in height, and allows the rope to pass under the feet twice before landing. The jumper should bend forward at the waist to help increase the speed of the rope. Advanced rope jumpers can be challenged to see how many consecutive double unders they can perform without stopping the rope.

"We do not want in the United States a nation of spectators. We want a nation of participants in the vigorous life."

*President John F. Kennedy*

# KEEPING CHILDREN PHYSICALLY FIT
## • TIPS FOR PARENTS •

Today's children are more sedentary than ever before. The Centers for Disease Control and Prevention recently reported that nearly half of the young people between the ages of 12 and 21 do not participate in regular daily exercise. They're also consuming more calories than ever before, mainly due to the high fat, high sugar content found in fast foods. The net result is that we have twice as many obese and overweight children as compared to 20 years ago. The social and economic consequences are enormous. The combination of inactivity and obesity puts a child at a far greater risk for many diseases later in adulthood, such as heart disease, high blood pressure, diabetes, etc. The President's Council on Physical Fitness and Sports reports that 40 percent of children as young as eight years of age show signs of at least one cardiac risk factor. In fact, very few conditions are not aggravated by excess weight and lack of exercise.

The need for parents to pay attention to their children's health habits is critical. Below are a few tips parents can use in promoting physical fitness and a healthier lifestyle for their children.

- Encourage children's fitness by setting a good example. Children learn many things from the role modeling exhibited by parents. If we want our children to be active and healthy, we need to be as well. Make physical activity a part of *your* everyday life–remember, little eyes are watching!

- Limit your child's time spent watching television, videos, movies, and computer games to less than two hours a day.

- Reduce the number of inactive family outings, such as going to a movie, and substitute more active outings like playing backyard games, hiking, biking, etc.

- Make exercise a social event. For example, birthday parties and special celebrations can be spent at a skating rink, bowling alley, etc.

- Give your children gifts that promote activity–a basketball, baseball glove, jump rope, frisbee, etc.

- Introduce your children to a variety of sports and activities and let them choose the ones they prefer. Exercise should be fun!

- Teach children movement skills at a young age. This includes throwing, catching, skipping, kicking, swinging, jumping, etc. A child who cannot play games will have a hard time staying fit.

# OUTCOMES & NATIONAL STANDARDS IN PHYSICAL EDUCATION

The National Association for Sport and Physical Education (NASPE) developed recommended physical education student learning standards when they published *Outcomes of Quality Physical Education Programs,* and a follow-up document titled *Moving into the Future: National Standards for Physical Education.* Together they provide physical educators with the guidelines for designing an appropriate K-12 curriculum. The author highly recommends these valuable documents for all home educators who teach physical education.

Below is a summary of the K-12 student outcome highlights. A physically educated person:

- Values physical activity and its contribution to a healthy lifestyle.

- Has learned the physical and cognitive skills necessary to perform a wide variety of physical activities.

- Has knowledge of the implications and benefits derived from participation in fitness-oriented activities.

- Achieves and maintains a health-enhancing level of physical fitness.

- Demonstrates responsible personal and social behavior in physical activity settings.

- Understands that physical activity provides opportunities for enjoyment, challenge, social interaction, and self-expression.

- Demonstrates an understanding and respect for differences among people in physical activity settings.

# INFORMATION & RESOURCES

## HELPFUL RESOURCES

Bailey, G. (2001). *The Ultimate Playground & Recess Game Book.* Camas, WA: Educators Press

Bailey, G. (2001). *The Ultimate Sport Lead-Up Game Book.* Camas, WA: Educators Press

Graham, G., S. Holt-Hale, and M. Parker. (1993). *Children Moving: A Reflective Approach To Teaching Physical Education.* 3d ed. Palo Alto, Calif.: Mayfield

Griffin, L., S. Mitchell, and J. Oslin. (1997). *Teaching Sport Concepts and Skills.* Champaign, IL: Human Kinetics

Landy, J. (2002). *P.E. Teacher's Pre-Sport Skill Lessons, Activities & Games for Grades 4-6.* Paramus, NJ: Parker Publishing

Launder, A. (2001). *Play Practice.* Champaign, IL: Human Kinetics

National Association for Sport and Physical Education (NASPE). *Developmentally Appropriate Physical Education Practices for Children.* Champaign, IL: Human Kinetics

National Association for Sport and Physical Education (NASPE). *Moving Into the Future: National Physical Education Standards.* Reston, VA: AAHPERD/NASPE

National Association for Sport and Physical Education (NASPE). *Outcomes of Quality Physical Education Programs.* Reston, VA: AAHPERD/NASPE

Pangrazi, R. (2001). *Dynamic Physical Education for Elementary School Children.* 13d ed. Boston, MA: Allyn & Bacon

Siedentop, D. (1994). *Sport Education: Quality PE Through Positive Sport Experiences.* Champaign, IL: Human Kinetics

Thomas, K.T., A.M. Lee, and J.R. Thomas. (2000). *Physical Education for Children.* Champaign, IL: Human Kinetics

# PHYSICAL EDUCATION ORANIZATIONS AND WEB SITES

- American Alliance of Health, Physical Education, Recreation & Dance,
  **www.aahperd.org/**

- State chapters of AAHPERD,
  **www.aahperd.org/**

- National Association for Sport and Physical Education,
  **www.aapherd.org/naspe/**

- National Association for Health & Fitness,
  **www.physicalfitness.org/**

- Project Fit America,
  **www.projectfitamerica.org/**

- PE Central,
  **www.pecentral.org/**

- American Alliance for Active Lifestyles and Fitness,
  **www.aapherd.org/aaalf**

- International Association for Sports Information,
  **http://sportquest.com**

- Spark,
  **www.foundationsdsu.edu/projects/spark/index.html**

- The President's Council on Physical Fitness and Sport,
  **www.fitness.gov**

- President's Physical Fitness Challenge,
  **www.indiana.edu/~preschal**

# INDEX
## (alphabetical by game)

**"Each day of our lives we make deposits in the memory banks of our children."**

*Charles R. Swindoll*

# ORDERING INFORMATION

Please contact your favorite bookstore or catalog company to order additional copies of *The Ultimate Homeschool Physical Education Game Book*. Customers can also order directly from Educators Press by using the contact information listed below. The retail cost is $19.95 per book plus $3.95 shipping (add $1 shipping for each additional book ordered). Washington state residents please add $1.40 per book for sales tax.

The following books are also available from Educators Press:

▸ **THE ULTIMATE PLAYGROUND & RECESS GAME BOOK**
ISBN 0966972724; $16.95 Retail Price

▸ **THE ULTIMATE SPORT LEAD-UP GAME BOOK**
ISBN 0966972732; $23.95 Retail price

Credit card purchases can be made through Educators Press by calling toll-free:

# 1-800-431-1579

Books from Educators Press are available at special discounts for bookstores, distributors, sales promotions, and premium sale programs. For details, contact the Sales Manager at Educators Press by telephone at (360) 834-3049, fax (561) 258-0554, or by email at educatorspress@att.net.

♦ ♦ ♦ ♦ ♦ ♦ ♦ ♦ ♦ ♦ ♦ ♦ ♦ ♦ ♦ ♦ ♦

**Educators Press**
**5333 NW Jackson Street**
**Camas, WA  98607**

**Tel. (360) 834-3049     Fax (561) 258-0554**
**www.educatorspress.com**